Arts: A Second Level Course

Renaissance and Reformation Units 17–19

Renaissance Music

Prepared by Gerald Hendrie and Dinah Barsham for the Course Team

The Open University Press

Part I   Gerald Hendrie and Dinah Barsham
Part II   Gerald Hendrie and Dinah Barsham
Part III Gerald Hendrie

The Open University Press
Walton Hall Milton Keynes
MK7 6AA

First published 1972. Reprinted 1973, 1976

Designed by the Media Development Group of the Open University.

Printed in Great Britain by
EYRE AND SPOTTISWOODE LIMITED
AT GROSVENOR PRESS PORTSMOUTH

SBN 335 00657 4

This text forms part of the correspondence element of an Open University Second Level Course. The complete list of units in the course is given at the end of this text.

For general availability of supporting material referred to in this text, please write to the Director of Marketing, The Open University, P.O. Box 81, Walton Hall, Milton Keynes, MK7 6AT.

Further information on Open University courses may be obtained from the Admissions Office, The Open University, P.O. Box 48, Walton Hall, Milton Keynes, MK7 6AB.

CONTENTS

Acknowledgements

The Working Group for Units 17–19 comprised: Trevor Bray, Francis Clark, Owain Edwards, John Ferguson, John Gilbert (BBC), Philip Olleson, Alasdair Clayre (BBC), Paul Kafno (BBC), Helen Rapp (BBC), Derek Rowntree, Peter Scroggs (BBC). We are indebted to them all for help and advice. Francis Clark counselled us wisely on the Reformation; Philip Olleson gave valuable help as Research Assistant and also compiled the Appendix; Trevor Bray transcribed and edited the music texts for Units 18 and 19 from original sources.

David Munrow acted as Consultant for Unit 17 and his specialist knowledge of both the practical and theoretical aspects of Medieval and Renaissance music proved invaluable to us.

Yet however much we owe to others, we bear responsibility for the overall plan of these units and any shortcomings they may exhibit.

G.H.   D.B.

Cover Illustration

Hans Holbein (1497–1543). *The Ambassadors* 1533. (82″ x 82¼″). Reproduced by courtesy of the Trustees of the National Gallery, London.

The ambassadors have been identified as Jean de Dinteville (1504–55), five times French ambassador or diplomatic envoy to England, and Georges de Selve (1508/9–41), ambassador to the Emperor, the Venetian Republic and the Holy See, and a friend of Dinteville who visited him in 1533.

The exact significance of the books and musical and astronomical instruments surrounding the two ambassadors is not known with any certainty: they were probably intended to convey learning in general rather than any more specific symbolism. On the lower shelf of the what-not can be seen a lute with a broken string (the case is on the floor below), a case of flutes and an open hymn book, which has been identified as an edition or derivative of Johann Walther's *Geystlich Gesangk Buchleyn* (Little Spiritual Songbook) first published in 1524. On the left-hand page is the first verse of the hymn *Komm heiliger Geist, Herr Gott* (Luther's reading of the Latin *Veni Creator Spiritus*), on the right the beginning of his 'Ten Commandments'. The other principal items on the what-not are as follows: on the lower shelf, a terrestrial globe and a half-open book of arithmetic: on the upper shelf, various astronomical instruments including a celestial globe, a portable sundial and a quadrant. The mosaic pavement is fairly closely derived from Abbot Ware's pavement at Westminster Abbey.

The distorted skull at the bottom of the picture is puzzling. It is probably a *memento mori*, but this leaves unexplained the distortion. It has been suggested that the picture was originally hung in such a position that one's first glimpse of it would be from below and to the left; from this vantage point the skull looks markedly less distorted. As the spectator approached the picture, the skull would become almost unrecognizable as such.

Philip Olleson

Preamble to Units 17–19

In this Renaissance and Reformation Course there are three correspondence units devoted to music, three radio programmes, two television programmes, and one gramophone record. The first correspondence unit introduces the subject of Renaissance music and then examines music and musicians in Renaissance society. We hope this will be of general rather than of specialist interest and have therefore tried to keep technical terms to a minimum. A section on Renaissance musical instruments and another on Renaissance musical forms conclude this unit, by way of preparation for the music you will hear in the broadcasts, and help to discuss in Units 18–19. These units deal respectively with vocal and keyboard music and they go hand in hand with the gramophone record. Texts of the music are provided in a supplement. An appendix at the end of Unit 19 contains a list of suggestions for further reading and listening as well as information about available editions of Renaissance music.

The first radio programme, presented by Professor Denis Arnold, is entitled 'Style and Idea in Renaissance Music' and considers the formative influences on Renaissance musical style; the second presents a variety of Renaissance Consort Music played by David Munrow and members of the Early Music Consort of London; in the third, Robert Tear (tenor) and Desmond Dupré (lute) illustrate a talk given by Dinah Barsham on a characteristic Renaissance form, the English lute-song. The first television programme deals with (mainly) secular vocal and instrumental music from England and Italy and it is again presented by David Munrow and the Early Music Consort of London. It was filmed in colour at Audley End, an early seventeenth-century house in Essex. The second television programme is concerned with English sacred music before and after the Reformation. It is presented by Gerald Hendrie and the musical examples are provided by the choir of New College Oxford under their director, Dr. David Lumsden.

Thus in Unit 17 we examine music's place in Renaissance life (which involves some of the effects of the Reformation on music), and we consider briefly the more important instruments and forms then in use. Units 18 and 19, supported by the gramophone record, focus on the music itself. The broadcasts bring further, varied Renaissance music to your ears and eyes.

We hope the whole block will initiate an understanding of, liking for, and an intuitive response towards Renaissance music for those at present unfamiliar with it, and will further illuminate areas which some of you have knowledge of already. But above all we hope it will stimulate your interest in what many music historians regard as a 'Golden Age' of music, and that you will find that this music speaks directly to you notwithstanding the four centuries or so that separate us from the men who composed, played, and first heard it.

UNIT 17   RENAISSANCE MUSIC PART 1

Introduction

If you studied the Arts Foundation Course you will remember Units 27 and 28, the short title of which was *Mendelssohn's Rediscovery of Bach*[1]. In this we touched on a number of matters arising from the performance of Bach's *St Matthew Passion* which the composer Felix Mendelssohn (1809–47) gave in Berlin on 11 March 1829. This was the first complete performance since Bach's death in 1750 and was exactly one hundred years later than Bach's own first performance. The most important long-term effect of Mendelssohn's remarkable performance – all seats were sold, a thousand people were turned away and two more performances of this huge work had to be arranged – was that for the first time many people became interested in earlier music. Hitherto, with certain exceptions of course, only contemporary music had interested them. Because of this renewed interest in music of the past – which coincided with the early nineteenth century's interest in the past generally – a new discipline arose, that of musicology, pursued by a new kind of musician, the musicologist. He was concerned with searching out old music, looking for good texts of it (autographs, authenticated copies and rare first editions) and presenting these in a way which facilitated modern performances. There was not only the musicologist's problem of editing the music, but also the performer's problem of how to play or sing it. A crucial problem was that earlier music had often been composed for instruments which were no longer in use, or without any instrumentation being specified, in forms that were no longer fashionable or familiar, and with performance-practices in mind which, although commonplace knowledge to a musician of its time, by the mid-nineteenth century were forgotten. In the first radio programme which accompanied the *Mendelssohn* units, Charles Cudworth discussed the way in which Handel's *Messiah* had been subjected to various and generally inflationary performances since it was first performed in 1742; and in the second television programme, 'The Right Instrument?', Gerald Hendrie investigated the above problem in terms of keyboard music by Bach (1685–1750) and Handel (1685–1759).

We would emphasize a few of the points we made in *Mendelssohn's Rediscovery of Bach*:

1   Until the mid-nineteenth century the only music widely performed was contemporary music; old music was ignored by all except historians of music.

2   In music, a change took place in the early nineteenth century – a renewed interest in the past spread from a few connoisseurs to a larger public. Mendelssohn's 1829 performance of Bach's *St. Matthew Passion* (1729) led the way towards a vigorous and disciplined study of earlier music.

3   The desire to perform earlier music confronted musicians with problems like the disappearance of old instruments and the unfamiliar practices of earlier performers. This in turn led to the question:

4   Should one attempt to give a performance such as the original composer intended (as far as it is possible to judge this) or should one re-create the music in terms familiar to the society of one's own time?

[1] The Open University (1971) Humanities: A Foundation Course, Units 27–28 *Mendelssohn's Rediscovery of Bach*, The Open University Press.

The remarkable thing about the turn of events of the past hundred and fifty years is that there has taken place an almost total reversal of the situation in which only contemporary music was performed. Today the vast majority of music (excluding jazz and pop) that we hear on radio, disc and in the concert-hall, is by dead rather than by living composers. Most of the music you see in a classical music shop is old music – Bach, Beethoven, Brahms and Debussy. Although the revival of interest in earlier music began in the nineteenth century and gathered force in the twentieth, it was only after the Second World War that the flood-gates were fully opened. A strong factor in this post-war enthusiasm was the advent of the long-playing gramophone record; the BBC's Third Programme contributed also, and was influential beyond Britain.

EXERCISE

Jot down in your notebook two or three musical results of the early nineteenth century's interest in the past.

(This illuminated drawing comes from the Tenor part of *Kyrie II* of Gheerkin's *Missa Panis quem ego dabo* (Mass: The bread which I shall give you) from the MS Cambrai 124 (sixteenth-century). Each time this picture occurs you should pause and make your response to the exercise.)

DISCUSSION

You probably mentioned the rise of the new discipline of musicology; the performance-problems that confronted musicians who wanted to revive earlier music; the assumption that earlier composers would have taken advantage of 'modern' developments, hence the 'inflationary' nature of many performances of early music; the change that has taken place in the last hundred and fifty years, whereby most music heard today is by non-contemporary composers; the question of whether 'authentic' performances are possible or desirable.

The eighteenth century was the first whose music achieved general popularity in the nineteenth and twentieth. The pre-eminence of Bach and Handel in music history rapidly became apparent. Bach's music had been kept alive by a handful of devoted admirers; Handel's music was better known largely because of the outstanding success of a handful of his works. *Messiah*, for example, was sung more or less annually by choral societies in Britain, a tradition which is still maintained. The harmonic idiom of the eighteenth century was not that far removed from that of the nineteenth or early twentieth, and although earlier composers might have been upset by the manner in which their works were now performed, their broad intentions were unlikely to be grossly misunderstood.

But the same is not true the further back in time we travel – and time-travelling became one of the chief pastimes of post-war musical audiences in the 1940s and '50s. The seventeenth century posed more problems than the eighteenth but at least the notation used by seventeenth-century composers was reasonably easy to understand. This is less true of the sixteenth century; indeed, before about 1550 notation was very different and transcription of such music is a specialized matter. Add to this the very real problems of what to do about forgotten instruments and performing-practices and you will understand why Renaissance music took longer to become widely known than music of the

Baroque or Classical periods.

At this point let us make clear what we are referring to in these units when we speak of Renaissance music. We mean Western music from about 1425 to 1600 – although in England the style we shall identify arrived late and lasted until about 1625. If you find the term 'Renaissance' inappropriate to music of the period you would not be wrong. The term is borrowed from art history where, as you will know by now, it has some relevance. Painters, sculptors and architects of the period, stimulated to some extent by discoveries of ancient works of art, saw in their own endeavours something of a renaissance or re-birth of the classical spirit they had come to admire so much. In music a similar movement developed in the theories and practices of the Florentine Camerata in the closing years of the sixteenth century; but paradoxically, the period these events inaugurated is referred to now as the 'Baroque era' – another term borrowed from art history where it was originally used as a term of abuse. Baroque means literally 'grotesque' or 'imbalanced' – the contrary of classical proportion, in fact. Yet, for convenience, we borrow art history's terms like 'Gothic', 'Renaissance', 'Baroque', 'Classical' and apply them to music.

Of course, it would be absurd to say that no one knew about Renaissance music until after 1945. Discerning musicians and others had specialist knowledge of it before then and such men were active in declaring its exceptional riches. Thus Sir Richard Terry (1865–1938), organist of Downside Abbey and later, from 1901–24, of Westminster Cathedral, edited much Renaissance music by English composers and was chairman of the editorial committee of *Tudor Church Music*, a critical edition of English church music in ten volumes. Among the members of that committee was a musicologist who contributed pre-eminently to our knowledge of the extraordinary richness of English Renaissance music, the Rev. Dr. Edmund Fellowes (1870–1951), a Canon of St. George's Chapel, Windsor Castle. The sheer volume of his published work in this field is prodigious: he edited thirty-six volumes of the *English Madrigal School*, the companion series *The English School of Lutenist Song-Writers*, and the complete music of William Byrd in twenty volumes. Fellowes also wrote the following books: *William Byrd*, *Orlando Gibbons*, *English Madrigal Verse* and *English Madrigal Composers*; and he published much else besides. And although Gustave Reese published his authoritative and encyclopaedic *Music in the Renaissance*[1] in 1954, he mentions in his preface that it took thirteen years to write – and obviously he could not have begun to write it without many years' close study of the subject. More recently, Thurston Dart, who until his early death in 1971 was King Edward Professor of Music at London University, added an extra dimension: that of live and recorded performances in which he was either harpsichordist or conductor, performing from texts he himself had produced. His book *The Interpretation of Music* deals with problems of musicology and performance-practice through the ages. In 1951, the year of the Festival of Britain, a new national collection of music called *Musica Britannica* was inaugurated and thirty volumes of English music have since appeared in that series, several of which are devoted to Renaissance music.

Thurston Dart's interest in musicology was largely fired by personal contact with the Belgian musicologist Charles van den Borren (1874–1966) whose enormous and varied output included *The Sources of Keyboard Music in England* (1913), a standard work dealing principally with Renaissance keyboard music. Many German scholars fled to America in the 1930s and by their own research and teaching stimulated remarkable interest there in early music. Much of this music is now published for the first time and probably enjoys a wider popularity than it did in its own day. Among the standard works by some of

[1] Details of many of the books referred to in the text can be found in Appendix I.

these scholars are *Music in the Middle Ages* (1940) and *Music in the Renaissance* (1954), both by Gustave Reese, and *Studies in Medieval and Renaissance Music* (1950) by Manfred Bukofzer (who wrote also *Music in the Baroque Era*, published in 1947). These books were all commissioned by W. W. Norton and Company of New York and their musical adviser at the time was Paul Henry Lang. Lang's own monumental *Music in Western Civilization* (1941) remains a landmark of musical scholarship. Willi Apel wrote *The Notation of Polyphonic Music 900–1600* and the *Harvard Dictionary of Music* and collaborated with Archibald Davidson to produce the *Historical Anthology of Music* (usually known as HAM) in two volumes, the first of which remains indispensable to students of Medieval and Renaissance music history since it presents texts and commentaries of much hitherto unobtainable music of those periods. The first four volumes of *The New Oxford History of Music* (*Ancient and Oriental Music; Early Medieval Music; Ars Nova and the Renaissance; The Age of Humanism*) are likewise invaluable to anyone seeking a detailed knowledge of the fields covered, and the third and fourth volumes are, of course, particularly relevant to a deeper study of later Medieval and Renaissance music.

All this is by way of introduction, for we want to bring two points to your attention. First, detailed knowledge of Renaissance music is of relatively recent date; and second, the Renaissance music that survives contains some of the best music ever composed. Remember too, that what survives is only the tip of the iceberg; much of it, especially the secular music, was never written down, and of the music that was notated, the greater part has been lost. Furthermore, tantalizingly little is known of the folk music of the period, the music enjoyed by those generally outside the orbit of the church or noble household. The 'high art' of the Renaissance, prolific and influential as it was, concerned a relatively small percentage of the European population. Folk art concerned far more, but since folk music was both passed down by oral tradition and partly improvised rather than notated, we shall never know much more than we can glean from passing contemporary references, song-texts, financial records (for specific duties) and visual records (paintings, wood cuts, and so on). Our attention in Units 17–19 is therefore concentrated on 'art music' – but we should not forget that this music was the music of a sophisticated minority.

At this point, a few words of caution are necessary. From the nineteenth century onwards, as more and more first-rate early music was uncovered, it became less possible to believe that there was an evolutionary process in art and that contemporary music was inevitably better than earlier music. The results were two-fold: more early music was performed, and less contemporary music. Today, as we have already noticed, the situation that had existed until around the mid-nineteenth century has been almost completely reversed. This in turn has resulted in a semi-breakdown of communications between the present-day composer and his musical audience to whom the language of modern music is now relatively unfamiliar and has also resulted in a loss of confidence in contemporary musical achievements.

EXERCISE

Why do you suppose present-day concert audiences prefer listening to music of past ages?

SPECIMEN ANSWER

A straightforward answer could be that during the last hundred years, although concert-goers have become increasingly aware of music of the past, they have nevertheless become somewhat entrenched in their tastes both with regard to specific composers and specific works. Moreover they have become used to the musical language of the past rather than the present and this has made them less adventurous in their attitude to contemporary music. 'New music' would mean to many such people music of the past they had not previously heard, rather than the new music of the present. Since concert-promotion is financially hazardous at the best of times, concert-managements tend to promote the 'safer' type of concert, comprising well-known successful works. The contemporary composer – unless unusually fortunate – finds little chance of success here and so may either migrate to more hospitable lands (film music, incidental music) or else become increasingly esoteric and introvert, writing for other professionals or even for his private satisfaction. The spiral continues.

It is at least arguable that the situation today is more extreme than hitherto and that a more deeply felt and widely held spirit of antiquarianism exists, and this by no means confined to the arts. Concern over preservation and conservation of heritage and resources now transcends national boundaries – even if appropriate action is not necessarily forthcoming. This concern is reflected in the smaller units of society from communities to individuals. It is no longer so easy to demolish a historic building; furniture and other domestic effects from even the quite recent past are sought with increasing awareness and perception of likely 'values'. Hardly anything escapes the antiquarian's net: cars, railway-stock, gramophone records, pre-war catalogues, uniforms, to mention only a few areas of interest. Whether this reflects society's primitive urge to hoard before catastrophe is impossible to tell: but certainly there would seem to be lacking in some quarters at least that buoyant optimism in contemporary achievements which, as we shall see, was a characteristic of Renaissance society.

Earlier we suggested that the musical language of the eighteenth century was not drastically different from that of the nineteenth. This was a deliberate over-statement since the harmonic language of the late nineteenth and earlier twentieth centuries did in fact undergo radical expansion. So did musical forms and instrumentation. But the point is that the musical language of eighteenth-century music can be understood in the same way that we can readily understand a novel by Jane Austen (1775–1817), although she used some words, phrases and constructions that are unfamiliar to us today. But reading Jane Austen is not like reading Chaucer (c. 1343–1400) whose vocabulary is so very different from ours. Something of the same problem exists when we go beyond Renaissance music and first hear Medieval music. Although a few of its sounds may have survived in later music, we may nevertheless feel disorientated and be unsure how to react to it.

Renaissance music, however, is 'modern' music – using the term modern in its widest sense. We can respond to it immediately, because its language, though different from that of later music, came to rely on many of the same basic principles, such as the controlled use of concord and discord – this, in particular, developed during the period. There arose a simple formula with respect to this control of concord and discord[1]:

[1] If you cannot hear or play this example and the next one, it would be a good idea for you to follow the Gibbons Fantasia on side 2 band 4 of your disc where such chord progressions occur (sometimes slightly ornamented) at bars 5-6, 8-9, 13-14, 16-17, 21-22, 30-31, 34-35, 37-38, 44-45. The Prelude on band 3 ends with the same chord progression, incidentally. Needless to say, similar progressions abound in the other music on the record.

(a) = *preparation*, that is, a concord on a weak beat, preparing for the forth-coming discord.

(b) = *discord* occurring on strong beat (if, as often happens, the 'discordant' note is tied over from (a) and not repeated, it is called a suspension).

(c) = *resolution* on weak beat.

And there arose towards the end of the period the principle of the supremacy of the key-note or tonic, together with its next-in-line the *dominant* or fifth note of the scale:

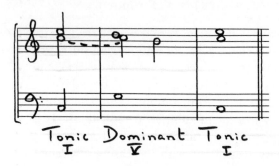

(Roman figures are often used to denote chord progressions.)

The enthusiastic response of modern audiences to Renaissance music proves that no natural barrier exists to prevent understanding and enjoyment of it; one can react to it intuitively in much the same way that one reacts to Beethoven, Brahms, or Tchaikovsky. But there still remains a basic difference between Renaissance music and the majority of nineteenth- and twentieth-century pieces heard today. This later music was usually composed as concert-music with an audience in mind. Most Renaissance music, on the other hand, was either functional (designed to enhance the liturgy, to accompany a procession, to serve as a backcloth to a banquet or other ceremony), or else was written with no audience in mind at all, since the performers were their own audience. The idea of sitting in silence in an auditorium while somebody else plays music to you, familiar enough to us and to our eighteenth- and nineteenth-century predecessors, would have seemed curious to anyone living before then. This functional aspect of Renaissance music and other early music is important – which is why we have decided to talk about it in this first unit, showing how forms, both sacred and secular, derived from the function required of the music. We shall deal too with Renaissance musical instruments, not exhaustively, but describing and illustrating the principal ones, how they were used together, and giving you an opportunity of hearing some of them on radio, television and the accompanying gramophone record. Let us begin, then, by considering the rôle of music and musicians in Renaissance society.

SECTION A
MUSIC AND MUSICIANS IN RENAISSANCE SOCIETY

In *Music in Western Civilization* (p. 297), Paul Henry Lang writes:

> Music occupied a position in the life of the man of the Renaissance and contributed to his intellectual wealth and social grace in a manner and degree which has not yet been taken into account by the historians of Western civilization. The idea of the time was the *uomo universale*, the universally educated man who, in the classical tradition, was a perfect physical specimen as well. To rear such a man a well-rounded musical education was considered indispensable. Baldassare Castiglione (1478–1529) in his *Libro del Cortegiano*[1], *The Book of the Courtier*, a treatise on etiquette, social problems and intellectual accomplishments, regarded as one of the great books of its time, devotes considerable attention to music in the education of well-bred people. It is, indeed, most interesting to notice the extraordinary vogue of music in the royal and princely courts during the Renaissance. Every monarch of note was interested in music, and many of them were capable players, singers or even composers.

All that is true enough and well documented. But note that Castiglione's *uomo universale* is an aristocrat. Castiglione is not concerned with the man in the street. Neither was Sir Thomas Elyot, whose *The Boke named the Governour* was published in 1531, three years after *The Book of the Courtier*, (though he, like Castiglione wrote in the vernacular, thus breaking the long tradition that Latin should be used for learned matters of all sorts). Castiglione's snobbery may not appeal to us today, and Elyot's intentions were hardly of concern to the man in the street since they were necessarily aimed at those who were concerned with the private upbringing of their sons; nevertheless there are definite liberal, 'educational' trends which make *The Governour* not only interesting to present-day readers but at times appear surprisingly up-to-date. Elyot aimed to produce well-equipped, well-balanced individuals who could later assume positions of responsibility and power, but use these with restraint and understanding for the well-being of others. In the last analysis therefore, Elyot's book is 'democratic', with a genuine desire to achieve a better life for the many through the careful education of the few.

To some extent this echoes Plato, as does Elyot's attitude to music. Music, concludes Elyot, is a powerful force that can affect the listener deeply. To be ignorant of music is a defect in a person. But to get too involved in it is equally dangerous – perhaps more so. It is better to be an aristocratic amateur than to display the kind of professionalism which could enable one to be mistaken for a genuine musician especially if that musician were a performer. Probably the best thing to aim for is sufficient critical knowledge to enable one to pronounce judgement on music and professional performances of it, without so to speak, soiling one's hands by direct participation. This Platonic attitude to music was not necessarily shared by Elyot's contemporaries: there is plenty of evidence of aristocratic involvement in both the composition and performance of music. In England, for example, Henry VIII had a professional knowledge of the composer's art – one which he put into practice from time to time – and his daughter Elizabeth had considerable talent as a keyboard performer. One of the most interesting composers in Italian Renaissance was a nobleman, Gesualdo, Prince of Venosa. Yet perhaps these were among the exceptions

---

[1] See Units 5–6 of this course, *The Mediaeval Inheritance and the Revival of Classical Learning*, Section 4.5. *The Book of the Courtier* is available as Penguin Classic L.192.

that would help to prove Elyot's rule: for since no monarch or prince could be mistaken for a professional musician, they could take as active a part as they liked in music's composition and performance. The readers of *The Governour* were not so highly privileged and for them Elyot's cautionary guidelines were probably necessary.

In Castiglione's Italy, therefore, the patron-consumer of secular music was likely to be an aristocrat acquainted with the theoretical and practical skills of music. Indeed, because of the existence of numerous rival states in Italy (see Unit 1, Section 32) patronage had always been more clearly in the hands of the individual noble who might or might not be a connoisseur of the arts – and there was no Reformation to alter this position. Many were such connoisseurs, as is shown by the achievements, especially musical, of the courts of the Medici, the Gonzaga, the Sforza and the d'Este families. In England, on the other hand, there was a single royal household associated with a single city, London, and in consequence patronage was centralized. The English royal family naturally wished to keep up with or excel their fellow monarchs abroad and to maintain a private chapel, choir, instrumentalists and resident composers was an effective and fashionable way of contributing to this end. Thus the royal musicians and their music had a central and privileged position in English musical life. It was to this one royal court that the best musical minds gravitated and there that the decisive changes of style and idea took place.

Throughout Europe, the Catholic church was still a major patron of sacred music. Yet her authoritarian influence was waning – for diverse reasons, many of which are discussed in Units 20–21 of this course, *Origins of the Reformation*. One reason had been that the struggle for the papacy and the existence of two popes in the fourteenth century – one at Rome, the other at Avignon – must have made it increasingly difficult for men to accept without question the dictates of an authoritarian religion. Also, the popes themselves were sometimes worldly and wealthy, a condition echoed in numerous lesser ecclesiastical establishments in which minor clerics found themselves by virtue of their education rather than any definite calling. One reason for the large number of worldly clerics in the fifteenth and sixteenth centuries was that the kind of education a boy received in a school attached to monastic establishments – education in music, grammar and Latin – while undoubtedly better than he would otherwise have received (if indeed, he would have received any at all) nevertheless fitted him for little else than to drift back into the system that had produced him and in which he could take minor holy orders. Such a person was unlikely to have the necessary social contacts to enable him to gain preferment into a noble household; even if possessed with exceptional natural ability, it would still be necessary for his talents to be observed and appropriate action to be taken. Records exist to show that minor clerics were frequently reprimanded for worldly vices – something that cannot have helped the church in her endeavour to maintain universal respect and discipline.

It is true that there was a certain revival of religious devotion in the hundred years between the Council of Constance of 1414–18 which ended the papal schism and Luther's nailing of his ninety-five theses to the church door at Wittenburg in 1517. Half a century later, the influence of the Counter-Reformation and the new undercurrents of the Baroque combined to produce the last and most glorious flowering of some two hundred years of compositional endeavour in the hands of four composers of exceptional renown: Palestrina (*c.* 1525–94) in Italy, William Byrd (1543–1623) in England, Orlandus Lassus or Orlando di Lasso (*c.* 1530–94) of the Netherlands, and Victoria or Vittoria (*c.* 1535–1611) of Spain.

At this point let us consider some of the effects on music and musicians of both the Reformation and the Counter-Reformation and see how they relate to the broader context of the Renaissance.

However much Lutheran, Calvinist, and other reformist theologies differed, they shared a common belief: the Word as revealed in Holy Scripture was central to the Christian Faith. The reformers considered an understanding of the Word a necessary qualification for salvation, hence their zealous concern that the Bible – which, in its Latin version was understood only by the better-educated priests or by scholars – should become readily available in vernacular translation. Such translation had important consequences beyond those directly relating to religious teaching. The way was paved for the production of further didactic works in the vernacular covering a variety of subjects previously the concern of professionals. Furthermore, as the vernacular became more widely printed so a standard form of it emerged largely free from dialect influence – this was especially true in England where the use of the vernacular was supported by a national liturgy. The *Word*, seen through vernacular translation, focused men's attention on the *word* – with far-reaching results.

Hitherto the clergy had used their professional skills to worship on behalf of their congregations, aided (or as some reformers argued, hindered) by music – also professionally performed. With the increasing use of the vernacular, however, the people 'found tho' late That what they thought the *Priest's* was *Their Estate*' (Dryden: *Religio Laici* – A Layman's Religion) and there resulted a growth of 'religious democracy' at the expense of 'religious professionalism'; so that in Germany, for example, when Luther provided his congregations with straightforward, memorable, stirring tunes and words to sing they responded wholeheartedly – as you can hear in the radio programme for Unit 23, 'The Music Explosion of the Reformation' by Dr. Erik Routley.

Music was not a prime concern of the reformers except insofar as it affected the teaching of the Word. Thus it was not so much the complex polyphony of the early sixteenth century that offended certain of them, but the fact that the texts of such music were sometimes doubly obscured – partly because they were not in the vernacular and partly because composers appeared to put musical considerations before those of clear verbal declamation. In this latter respect the Protestant reformers who – like Luther and Cranmer – were well-disposed towards music adopted a position towards it not far removed from that of the Catholic Reformers at the Council of Trent (1545–63), who, on 10 September 1562 worded a canon dealing with music to be used at Mass. Gustave Reese in *Music in the Renaissance* (p. 300) quotes from it in translation:

> In the case of those Masses which are celebrated with singing and with organ, let nothing profane be intermingled, but only hymns and divine praises. The . . . singing . . . should be constituted not to give empty pleasure to the ear, but in such a way that the words may be clearly understood by all, and thus the hearts of the listeners be drawn to the desire of heavenly harmonies, in the contemplation of the joys of the blessed . . . They shall also banish from church all music that contains, whether in the singing or in the organ playing, things that are lascivious or impure.

Luther, a knowledgeable amateur of music, able to perform and compose, was aware of the value of music as an aid to worship and would no doubt have concurred with the pronouncement of the Council of Trent. In addition to admitting the use of polyphony (even with instrumental accompaniment) in the reformed service he was content to retain the plainsong melodies of the Catholic church. In his preface to Johann Walther's *Geystlich Gesangk Buchleyn* (Little Spiritual Songbook),[1] a collection of religious part-songs, he wrote

---

[1] Which you can see on the cover of these units and which is described inside.

'I would see all the arts, and more particularly music, at the service of Him who created them and gave them to us'. Not so Zwingli, Calvin and other leaders of the non-Lutheran Protestant churches, who, as you will see in Units 24–25 adopted a more 'puritan' attitude to church music, art, and other external aids to devotion, most of whom opposed the retention of 'popish' practices. Furthermore – unlike Luther again – they generally opposed the singing of texts not found in the Bible. Effectively this confined them to the psalms, which they had translated into rhymed, metrical versions and set to newly-composed or traditional tunes.

In England, the Act of Supremacy of 1534 proclaiming Henry 'the only supreme head in earth of the Church of England' severed ties with Rome. Two years later the wholesale redistribution of church property began. Within four years over eight hundred monastic foundations were dissolved – about fifty of which maintained skilled choirs, according to Peter le Huray in *Music and the Reformation in England*. Large numbers of musicians lost their livelihoods as a result of the suppression of the monasteries and were forced to seek other, often secular, possibly non-musical employment. The death of Henry VIII in January 1547 and the accession of Edward VI, then nine years old, opened the way to more ardent reform under Protector Somerset. (You will learn more of this in Units 24–25, and will find Chapter 4 of your set book *The Reformation* by Owen Chadwick[1] particularly helpful.) The suppression of the chantries in 1547 had even more damaging consequences for music. (A chantry was an endowed chapel in which Masses were said or sung for the repose of the benefactor's soul.) Many of the chantries had been lavishly endowed and had maintained choirs whose composers were prominent within the polyphonic tradition. Notwithstanding certain exemptions – chantries within the Universities of Oxford and Cambridge, St. George's Windsor, Winchester and Eton colleges – the Chantries Act affected English music seriously, not least, as we shall consider later, in matters of education. Further injunctions sought to erase 'popish' memories: thus many saints' days and other holy days were abolished, images and relics destroyed together with rood-lofts, organs and Latin service books. Despite these events Henry VIII's reign saw little in the way of liturgical reform. In 1543 lessons at morning and evening service were appointed to be read in English. Sermons became more common. The Communion service was soon to be celebrated in English, and musical settings were adapted or newly composed.

It might be expected that the publication of the First Prayer Book of Edward VI (*The Book of Common Prayer*), authorized to replace all existing books necessary for the divine services, would have clarified prevailing attitudes to music. It did nothing of the sort however, at least not explicitly. Not a note of music appeared in it, unlike the Latin books it had supplanted, and no instructions relating to music were given. Yet some of the early reformers were sympathetic to music and musically inclined. The absence of musical guidelines in the new prayer book can hardly have been an oversight or the result of indecision. It is possible that it was assumed that music would play a substantial part in the reformed services as it had done before; or else perhaps the attitude to music of other reformers had hardened sufficiently by 1549 for this assumption to be unwarranted – in which case the absence of a specific rubric forbidding music would seem curious, admittedly, unless explained in terms of good public relations. Perhaps there was, even among less sympathetic reformers, a genuine reluctance to inflict further damage on the English choral tradition. As we have already noted, the suppression of the monasteries and chantries had resulted in numerous skilled choirs being disbanded and their members seeking other

[1] Chadwick, O. (1964) *The Reformation*, Penguin (set book).

employment. Further losses would have put in jeopardy a tradition whose excellence had long been acknowledged at home and abroad.

Of the two new services contained in the prayer book, distilled from eight Latin ones, Matins (or Mattins) contained a single reference to music at the Venite which is directed to be 'said or sung' and Evensong contained an oblique reference to music at 'the Clerks [lay-clerks or choirmen] kneeling'. Both references would seem to favour the thesis that music's part in the new services was to be taken for granted. ('Venite' and other such terms are discussed in the section on musical forms.)

In 1552 a more radical Second Prayer Book was issued offering somewhat fewer opportunities for composers. However, Anglicanism was temporarily halted the following year, for Edward died and his sister Mary succeeded him, restoring full communion with Rome and reviving Latin rites. This proved to be but a brief return to Catholicism for in 1558 Elizabeth succeeded Mary and the following year an Elizabethan Act of Uniformity was passed restoring the 1552 prayer book with a few more conservative re-touchings. An accompanying Royal Injunction of 1559 had important musical consequences: it was allowed that 'in the beginning or in the end of Common prayers, either at Morning or Evening, there may be sung a hymn or suchlike song'. This led to a particularly English musical phenomenon, the anthem, which can be defined no more specifically than as a composition involving voices intended for use in the Anglican church. It could be short or long, simple or complex, unaccompanied or accompanied, with a liturgical or non-liturgical text. Yet the anthem, by virtue of the lack of any constraint other than fitness for its function (implicit in the Injunction which continued: 'having respect that the sentence [meaning] of the Hymn may be understood and perceived') took root, flourished, and became a source of inspiration to composers of succeeding generations.

Those who like their facts cut and dried should avoid the subject of English church music of the mid-sixteenth century for it involves too many loose ends. For example, an unidentified piece of music with English text may have been newly composed following the introduction of the First Prayer Book of 1549; or it may have been written a short while previously to facilitate a smooth change-over from Latin to English rites; or else it may have been adapted from an altogether earlier piece of Latin church music; or, just possibly, it may have been composed for a celebration *in English* of a Roman office. On the other hand, a musical setting of a Latin text may be either pre- or post-Reformation, since the old Catholic worship was the State religion between 1553 and 1558. (Indeed, there appeared in 1560 a translation into Latin of the *Book of Common Prayer*, Haddon's *Liber Precum Publicarum*, which was approved by Royal Injunction for use at Oxford and Cambridge.) Furthermore, leading composers like Tallis (*c.* 1505–85) and Byrd (1543–1623) both Gentlemen of the Chapel Royal, continued throughout their long lives to compose Latin church music alongside their English church music. Queen Elizabeth appears to have condoned such apparently anomalous behaviour amongst distinguished persons: she described one of Byrd's patrons, the Earl of Worcester, as 'a stiff papist and a good subject'; and although Byrd himself was cited three times for recusancy no serious consequences ensued. Elizabeth had her own personal policy, it seems, distinguishing recusancy from treason.

Concerning the actual sacred music that appeared around the middle of the century and in the years immediately following, there were of course two sorts fulfilling two separate functions: that produced for congregational or domestic use (and therefore printed) and that intended for professional use by trained choirs (and therefore often circulated in manuscript copies). Examples of publications belonging to the first category are Miles Coverdale's short-lived

Ghoostly Psalmes and Spirituall Songs, and *Psalms in English Metre*. John Marbeck's *The Booke of Common praier noted* belongs to the same category. Marbeck set the texts to simple plainsong-like melodies, more-or-less one note to a syllable – as Cranmer, in a letter of 1544 to Henry VIII, had suggested would be fitting for his own English litany. Marbeck's solution was pleasing and apparently acceptable, but the work only ran to one printing, no doubt because of the revisions contained in the 1552 book, and because of the lack of enthusiasm for unison congregational singing. Nevertheless Marbeck's 'noting' of the Communion is still used today in some churches. The *Actes of the Apostles* by Christopher Tye (*c.* 1500–73) is an example of part-music intended for domestic use. Tye made a metrical version of fourteen chapters of the Acts in a simple, largely homophonic style, though with a little imitation. One movement, with altered words, remains in common use today and serves as an easy anthem. It is *O come ye servants of the Lord*, and it provides a good example of the straightforward, syllabic, and tuneful style favoured by the reformers:

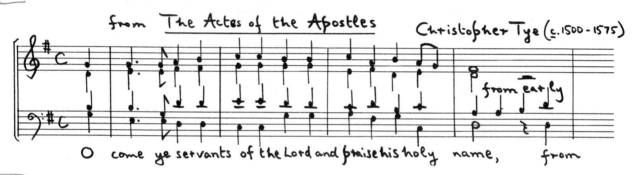

Psalters, you will remember, were rhymed metrical versions of the psalms set to music, intended both for congregational use and for private devotion. In 1562 Day published the chief Anglican psalter *The Whole Booke of Psalmes* of Sternhold and Hopkins 'with apt Notes to synge them withal' and the following year a version with four-part musical settings, *Whole psalmes in foure partes*. This collection included a tune known later as the Old Hundreth (because the hundreth psalm was set to it) still in familiar use today together with its associated text. Uncompromising yet persuasive, it is typical of the best psalter tunes at home and abroad:

(Psalm 100, Prayer Book version: O be joyful in the Lord all ye Lands: serve the Lord with gladness and come before his presence with a song.)

Other psalters followed Day's: for example Archbishop Parker's of about 1567 (a very small edition) with nine original tunes by Thomas Tallis, including that on which Vaughan Williams based his *Fantasia on a Theme by Tallis* for string orchestra of 1910; several in the 1580s and '90s, and lastly Ravenscroft's of 1621. A number of today's best-known Anglican hymn-tunes first appeared in these psalters.

Anglican church music for choir rather than congregation falls into two categories: services, that is, settings of the appropriate parts of Matins, Evensong and the Communion; and anthems, already mentioned. Services and anthems were at first simple and largely homophonic – somewhat after the style of Tye's *Actes*. Certainly, when compared with pre-Reformation music they show the Reformation's influence clearly enough. Look at the following two music examples, both of which pieces you will hear and see in the second television programme. Notice how different they appear on paper: the first is rich and ornate, and far from being set 'for every syllable a note'. The second is simple, economical and almost entirely syllabic. Provided it is sung clearly the listener cannot fail to 'perceive and understand'. Yet Tallis did not write such music because of limited skill – he was among the greatest poly-phonists of his age as we shall see later. (You will also hear the above-mentioned psalm-tune by Tallis in the television programme – indeed the broadcast is directly relevant to this whole section on English church music.)

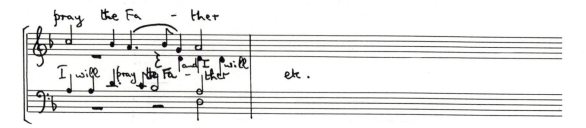

Interruption

Although it is unnecessary to memorize the details of the preceding section on the Reformation and its effect on English church music and musicians, you should try to retain an overall picture of it. The following exercise should help you in this.

EXERCISE

Note briefly five musical effects in England of the Reformation.

SPECIMEN ANSWER

(Choose any five statements.)

1 Numerous disestablished church musicians sought secular employment.
2 The use of the vernacular in musical settings of parts of the liturgy.
3 Increased congregational participation in the reformed services combined with increased comprehension of the liturgy.
4 Adoption by the reformers of Calvinist rather than Lutheran attitudes to music.
5 The implicit rather than explicit opportunities offered by the 1549 prayer book.
6 The publication of psalters, Day's of 1562 and 1563 being particularly important.
7 Simpler sacred music, with more syllabic setting of the text.
8 The Royal Injunction of 1559 allowing that a 'hymn or suchlike song' be sung at Matins and Evensong. Hence, the anthem.

With the musical principles established during the Reformation in Germany, England, and other affected countries and the adoption of those principles in Luther's own chorale melodies, Walther's *Geystlich Gesangk Buchleyn*, Marbeck's *Booke of Common praier noted*, Tye's *Actes of the Apostles*, and in numerous compositions in all the reformed countries, it might seem that polyphony in sacred music was well and truly subdued. Yet as soon as the wind of reform was no longer so chill, polyphony began to stir once again, at first timidly and then with increasing vigour. Finally, around the turn of the century, under an unexpected combination of favourable circumstances, it flowered in a truly remarkable manner. These favourable circumstances were: the Counter- or Catholic Reformation, whose influence gave a new impetus to religious art both in Catholic countries and also in those previously dominated by the Protestant ethic but now susceptible to the influence of the Counter-Reformation; and the exhilarating, heady influence of the early Baroque. Needless to say, the Catholic Reformation, the fading of the Renaissance and the beginnings of the Baroque overlapped and interacted.

Thus in Italy, Palestrina devoted his life to the service of the church and under the influence of the Counter-Reformation his genius found full expression in the sacred polyphony of Mass and motet. Victoria, probably Palestrina's pupil, and certainly his successor at the Seminary (see Unit 18), returned in his forties to his native Spain; his polyphony combines mystical intensity with a typically Spanish sense of drama. Lassus and Byrd, two other musical giants, served the church with hardly less devotion. Where the influences of Counter-Reformation and Baroque combined they seemed to produce larger-than-life works of art. Thus Byrd's 'Great Service' is a truly great work both in scale and in historical importance. Tallis's vast forty-part motet *Spem in alium nunquam habui* (I never had hope in other than Thee) would have remained a museum-piece were it not that the trials of organization and rehearsal are forgotten in performance, so triumphantly does the outcome justify the means.

But it was in Germany that the most remarkable development took place. Martin Luther had shown greater psychological perception in his attempt to found a Protestant musical culture than had his fellow reformers elsewhere. German musicians found the Lutheran chorale congenial from the outset, and particularly well-suited to polyphonic arrangement either in a simple or an elaborate manner. Protestantism of the Swiss tradition was unsympathetic to the arts, but in Germany Luther contrived to found an incomparable musical culture. The Lutheran chorale was to provide the highest inspiration for the music of the next two centuries. In the period with which we are now concerned, the turn of the seventeenth century, among the numerous chorale-inspired works were those with Italian influences also, which again seemed to produce larger-than-life results: one such was *Musae Sionae* (Songs of Sion) of 1605-10 by Michael Praetorius (1571-1621) comprising no less than 1,244 chorale-inspired compositions, ranging from simple four-part pieces to elaborate ones in eight to twelve parts in the Venetian style. Michael Praetorius was also the author of *Syntagma Musicum* (Treatise of Music) of 1615-20, from the second volume of which some of our illustrations in the following section on musical instruments are taken.

The chorale's influence on German composers of the seventeenth and eighteenth centuries culminated in that of J. S. Bach (1685-1750), a great deal of whose music the chorale pervades in fact or in spirit. It is no exaggeration to say that the Lutheran chorale became to Protestantism what Gregorian chant had long been to Catholicism. This was the Lutheran contribution to music and to the Renaissance.

It was fitting that our brief discussion of music and the Reformation should have begun and ended with Luther, for he was the pioneer of the Reformation and, as we have seen, he was also the founder of a Protestant musical culture. We began our discussion too, with a consideration of the importance the reformers attached to the *Word* and we suggested, somewhat cryptically, that this led men to a closer regard for the *word*. Let us then leave the Reformation and pursue this line of thought in the wider context of the Renaissance.

The Renaissance composer's attitude to the relationship of text and music is perhaps what distinguishes him most clearly from his Medieval predecessors. This is argued at some length in John Stevens' *Music and Poetry in the Early Tudor Court*, a book as remarkable for its lucidity as for its scholarship. By and large, Medieval composers subscribed to the view of music expressed by Boethius (executed about 525) in his *De Institutione Musica* (Concerning musical education) and which you have met already in Units 5–6, Section 6.3. Briefly, Boethius took a philosophical-mathematical viewpoint, defining a musician as one whose approach to music was *beneficio speculationis*, 'through the good gift of thought'. This view sustained musical theory for nearly a thousand years – in fact there were a number of reprints of Boethius in Venice in the closing years of the fifteenth century and it was from these that musicians of the sixteenth century drew their information. Dr. Stevens observes: 'significantly, the difference between a musician and a mere performer was thought to be the same as between a *theologus* [theologian] and *recitor* [lesson-reader]. It is not a surprise to find the *summus ille musicus* [the supreme musician] is Christ himself' (p. 59).

Earthly music, then, was a reflection of the music of the universe – which explains the importance of numbers in Boethian musical theory (conveniently reinforced by the scientific basis of music, first identified by the Greeks) and also accounts for music's place alongside mathematics in the Medieval *quadrivium* (see Units 5–6, Section 4.1). It explains too, why the complicated system of proportional notation and other mathematical constructional devices were so favoured by Medieval composers. Yet given the rhythmical constraints to which any single voice-part was bound within such a medieval composition, it is hardly surprising that the words sometimes appear to have been fitted to the music almost as an afterthought.

Boethian musical theory remained the cornerstone of a number of Renaissance treatises on music – of the Swiss mathematician Glareanus' *Dodecachordon* (Instrument of twelve strings) of 1547, for example – despite the growing preoccupation of Renaissance composers with the *word* and their awareness of the *expressive* potentialities of a musical style in which the word, not the music, was the more dominant partner. Once this last principle was established, musical composition was no longer a primarily intellectual activity, but became instead an expressive art in which heart and mind combined freely.

Among the first of the progressive composers of the Renaissance – and, incidentally, one of the outstanding composers of all time – was a Netherlander, Josquin des Près (1450–1521) whose compositions show great sensitivity to their texts. Towards the middle of the sixteenth century more definite trends towards 'word painting' are found: thus individual phrases, individual words even (like 'sigh', 'high', 'low', 'heaven', 'hell') were treated semi-literally while more 'difficult' words like 'darkness' or 'light' were sometimes denoted by the use of black or white notation; and since such a device would be evident only to the performers, it introduced a kind of performers' freemasonry. Something similar existed, by the way, in the sacred music of certain mid-sixteenth-century composers (for example Jacob Clement *c.* 1510–*c.*1556) where daring effects might be achieved in the performance of a particular passage by the introduction of unwritten accidentals, the possibility of, and necessity for which, would become apparent to the singers only in course of performance. The notated music would thus appear pure and unexceptional: certainly its secrets would be undetectable to any cleric seeking signs of unseemly innovation. There may perhaps have been nobler motives for this concealment – it remains one of music's mysteries.

Two important progressive groups should be mentioned here, both of which looked to antiquity for guidance: the *Académie de Musique et de Poèsie* (Academy of Music and Poetry) of Paris, founded in 1575 with the aim of uniting the arts of music and poetry; and the *Camerata* (Friends) of Florence, who met in the last decade of the century and sought to revive the principles of Greek music and drama. The former initiated a new musical style known as *vers mesurée* (measured verse), based on the classical metrical system of 'long' and 'short' syllables (involving the length of time taken to pronounce the syllable: if *to* is matched with ♪ then *too* might be matched with ♩) rather than stress or accent. The resulting music was rather plain and chordal but it did reflect the declamation of the text very precisely. The principal composer of *vers mesurée* was Claude le Jeune (1528–1600). The Camerata comprised men of letters, poets, singers and musical theorists. Strongly opposed to polyphony, they devised a simple, vocal, expressive music (called monody) which sought to capture every nuance of the text and whose accompaniment was almost exclusively chordal. These experiments led to the most important single event in the history of music: the birth of opera.

Hitherto unaccompanied part-singing had probably been a rare thing in music and then a result of necessity rather than of design, as for example, in the somewhat stylized outdoor vocal group shown below.

Figure 1 Unaccompanied Singers. Anonymous, fifteenth century (Bourges Museum).

There is evidence that vocal music was normally supported by one or more instruments. Yet although monody required instrumental accompaniment, composers striving to express every nuance of a text in a madrigal (a piece for several voices having a particularly close correspondence of text and music) in all probability no longer wanted this inevitable instrumental support. This lack of dependence of vocal music on instruments went hand in hand with advances being made at this time in instrumental design. The Medieval organ, for example, was either large and unwieldy to play, or else small, portable, and really only capable of playing a melodic line (however highly ornamented) because the player used his left hand to work the bellows. The Renaissance organ, on the other hand, was more flexible and, like the Renaissance harpsichord, enabled a solo performer to play tune *and* accompaniment or else polyphony. The lute was the Renaissance instrument *par excellence*, capable of almost any demands made on it either as a solo, or as an accompanying instrument. Melodic instruments such as recorders were made in large families, yielding an independent ensemble of homogeneous tone-quality.

Lack of desire for inevitable instrumental support in certain word-conscious Renaissance compositions and the advances of Renaissance instrumental design combined to give rise to a phenomenon which later generations have taken for granted: instrumental music. There was relatively little purely instrumental music before the Renaissance. However, we shall refer to these matters again in the section on musical instruments.

Beyond doubt, one of the most important factors in musical development in the sixteenth century was the advent of music printing. A few sporadic attempts had appeared in the late fifteenth century, but it was Petrucci of Venice who in 1501 produced the first substantial and wholly satisfactory music printing. During the next twenty years he published over fifty volumes of supremely beautiful work. These music books would have been sufficiently costly to preclude all but the wealthier connoisseurs from buying them, so again we are reminded of the aristocratic nature of Renaissance culture. (Petrucci's work was expensive for several reasons: it was innovatory; it was artistic; but above all, vocal music had to be triple-impressed, that is, it went through the presses three times, once to print the music-staves, once for the notes to be superimposed, and a third time so that the text could be added.) In 1525 Pierre Attaingnant of Paris introduced the first single-impression printing from movable type, less attractive than Petrucci's work, but also much less expensive. Shortly afterwards this method spread to Germany, the Netherlands, and back to Italy. As music-printing became less complicated and less of a rarity, it became cheaper, and caused one of the great revolutions in music. Manuscript copies of music were costly and necessarily precious. Large manuscripts, written on parchment and often painstakingly illuminated, were evidently kept primarily for reference and copying purposes, judging from the exceptionally fine state of many which survive. True, the larger manuscripts may have been used for performance as some contemporary pictures indicate. Such pictures show a group of musicians gathered around a lectern all singing from the single copy, but in the miniature dating from around 1530 of the composer Johannes Ockeghem (*c.* 1430–95) and his singers, it is clear that the large manuscript is being treated with respect. More usually, performing parts were made from these reference copies, often on paper, but these have either been lost or have simply fallen apart with frequent use. Indeed what would be the most interesting evidence of all, the composer's autograph, seldom exists at all, since apparently he composed on a *cartelle*, a ruled sheet of parchment incised with stave-lines, which could be wiped clean after a new work had been composed and copied. No such cartelle is known to have survived although there is evidence that cartelles existed.

Cheaper printed music brought a new, less-than-aristocratic public literally in touch with music for the first time. A natural consequence was a spate of publications intended for domestic consumption by reasonably talented middle-class amateurs. This was reinforced by the Reformation's encouragement of domestic religious activity, and particularly in countries affected by Calvinism, in the singing of psalms. Psalters appeared in increasing numbers during the second half of the sixteenth century. The principal French Psalter was published in its final form in 1562 with music arranged or composed by Louis Bourgeois (*c.*1510–*c.*1561), some of whose splendid, memorable tunes are still in current use today. Translations of the French Psalter appeared in Germany, Holland, England and Scotland. The most important English Psalter, as we noted earlier, was that of Sternhold and Hopkins, of 1562 and 1563, and a Scottish Psalter appeared in 1564. All these were used both in church and in the home.

Secular music, vocal and instrumental, was published in increasing quantities. The title-page might even state 'apt for voices or viols' ('to be sung or played') probably to assist sales rather than expressly reflecting the composer's wishes, however. Many textbooks were published too, both on musical theory and on instrumental playing, demonstrating a demand for self-improvement among amateurs and doubtless some professionals too.

Of the instrumental treatises, Silvestro Ganassi's *La Fontegara* (literally perhaps 'The rivalry of origin' – but it doesn't really respond to translation), published in Venice in 1535, is the earliest known recorder method; while Thomas Morley's *A Plain and Easy Introduction to Practical Music* of 1597 – in actual fact, scarcely plain and far from easy – ranks among the most important theoretical treatises. (Notwithstanding its title, Morley's work is largely concerned with theory.) Remembering that Glareanus, Morley and other Renaissance authors who set out to write a treatise on the theory of music were hidebound by what had been written previously, all of which repeated what Boethius had said Plato had said, we should not be surprised at the dichotomy which existed between Renaissance musical theory and practice.

By the end of the sixteenth century music printing was a thriving concern. Thurston Dart points out in his introduction to the modern reprint[1] of *A Plain and Easy Introduction* that in London, Thomas East, who in 1587 had taken over part of the music printing monopoly held previously by William Byrd and Thomas Tallis, by 1593 had printed more music books than had been published during the previous eighty years altogether. East also published a Psalter in 1592, and in particular, madrigals by Thomas Morley. With Morley's madrigals he inaugurated the English Madrigal School which was (to quote from Dart's same foreword) 'perhaps the most splendid thirty years in the whole history of English music'.

We have mentioned music and music tutors intended for the intelligent amateur, whose musical education must have increased enormously during this period as a result. But what of musicians' own education during this period?

In England, before the suppression of religious houses and the dissolution of the monasteries, choristers who assisted at monastic services received musical education and some general education at the attached song schools. The 1547 Chantries Act inflicted more serious damage, but as we have already seen made provision for important exemptions: thus at Oxford and Cambridge, chapels and song schools flourished, as did also those at Windsor, Winchester and Eton. As we would expect, many eminent musicians flourished there. Orlando Gibbons (1583–1625), for example, an outstanding Renaissance composer and performer, began his musical education as a choirboy at King's College Cambridge where his elder brother was organist. Thomas Weelkes (*c.* 1575–1623), composer of sacred and secular vocal music, was Organist of Winchester College in the late 1590s. Nevertheless, the dissolution of the monasteries and the abolition of their song schools deprived many children of a musical education. True, some might be fortunate enough to go to grammar

[1] See Appendix I for details.

school instead and certain grammar schools made healthy provision for the teaching of music: for example, Westminster, Christ's Hospital, Dulwich, Merchant Taylor's and St. Paul's – whose founder had been Dean Colet, one of the 'Oxford Reformers' and friend of Erasmus.

In England the highest standards of musical instruction – as of performance and composition – were attained under royal patronage, either in the Royal Chapels or among the 'Kings Music'. This was hardly surprising for as we have already noted, there was offered a degree of centralized patronage unique in Europe. The best church musicians sought employment in the Chapel Royal (the best boy-choristers in the country being pressed into service there by royal prerogative) while their instrumental colleagues vied with each other for a place in the King's Music. The Gentlemen of the Chapel Royal were predominantly English – as would be expected in view of their singing-duties – but many of the King's Music were foreign as can readily be seen from names like Bassano, Lupo and Ferrabosco. Furthermore music, like any other skill, was kept very much within the family in the Renaissance and nowhere more so than among the members of the King's Music. The Bassano family worked at the English court from 1538 to 1641; the Lupos from 1540 to 1640; similarly the Ferraboscos, father and son. Such families would pass on their music, instruments and appointments from father to son.

At university music was part of the Medieval curriculum (as we have seen in Units 5–6) and as already mentioned here, it was the academic or theoretical aspects that were studied, not the practical skills. A diet of Boethius cannot have been very exciting however, and fortunately there arose during the fifteenth century a more cheerful aspect of English university music, namely the institution of music degrees (Bachelor and Doctor of music) in which composition was the prime discipline. Admittedly, the Bachelor's degree at Cambridge does not seem to have involved composition at first, but it did later, and the Doctor's degree seems always to have been a composer's degree – and still is, for that matter. Although it is arguable that a good composer, then as now, should find his own level regardless of a music degree, the degree nevertheless offered a guarantee of musicianship helpful both to a prospective employer and to its recipient within his own professional circle. The universities did not grant such degrees easily for the requirements were stringent. The earliest Cambridge Doctor of Music degree appears to have been awarded not later than 1463 to a now obscure musician. Oxford followed much later, in 1511, conferring the degree on the celebrated composer Robert Fayrfax, who had already taken his Doctorate at Cambridge seven years previously. Fayrfax (c. 1460–1521) was a Gentleman of the Chapel Royal by 1496, and later organist of St. Albans Abbey. Both sacred and secular vocal music by him survives and his spacious, lengthy, slow-moving yet complex polyphony is wonderfully suited to the building for which it was written. Many, if not most, of the important English composers of the Renaissance held music degrees.

We have stressed already the emphasis religious reformers placed on the use of the vernacular in worship in place of the traditional Latin. We must not forget that all university education was in Latin too, and although this meant that a scholar could transfer from one university to any other with ease regardless of national boundaries, it may have proved something of a stumbling-block to the introduction of new ideas. (Old traditions die hard, incidentally: Cambridge University abolished Latin as an entrance requirement in 1961, Oxford University in 1971.)

Admittedly Dr. John Bull (1563–1628), the eminent composer and keyboard virtuoso, was permitted to give his twice-weekly lectures on music in English at Gresham's College, London (founded in 1596 by provision of Sir Thomas

Gresham's will) – yet the exception made in Bull's case 'because at this time Dr. Bull is recommended to the place by the queen's most excellent majesty not being able to speak Latin'[1] serves to underline the prevailing tradition.

Although it was possible to receive a good university music education in theory and composition, nothing existed in England like the present Royal Academy of Music (1823) or Royal College of Music (1883) – institutions founded primarily to give first-rate instrumental education, although of course, theory and composition are taught in addition. To receive instrumental instruction in Renaissance England it was necessary to become apprenticed to a member of the nearest instrumental guild – the waits – in exactly the same way as in any other trade. The Royal Waits were a very tight-knit group as we have seen; but the provincial waits were less so, though still sharing the influence of the 'family trade' – as, of course, would also have been the case with other occupations. (There is still a natural tendency for professions to run in families but perhaps this tendency remains stronger in music, the theatre and the arts in general. This is presumably not because of the easy life they offer, but because of the large amount of semi-intuitive background knowledge that can be acquired in childhood in these fields together with the absolute necessity in music to acquire instrumental proficiency at an early age.)

Not all secular musicians in England were employed in noble establishments. There were also the waits employed by civic authorities. (Orlando Gibbons' father was a member of the Cambridge waits)[2]. The term was applied originally to those who watched at the gates of a town, especially during hours of darkness, and who communicated approaching danger by means of loud instruments. But their function became less protective and more musical during the Renaissance and their range of instruments and activities increased accordingly. Many towns possessed one or more waits and among many contemporary records of their activities, vestiges of their earlier functions appear fairly regularly. The records for Ipswich provide an instance of this, as Woodfill points out in his chapter on the waits in *Musicians in English Society*. He refers (p. 75) to the order appointing a certain John Betts and his company in 1597–8 which prescribes that they

> shall walk about the town with their waits from Michaelmas until our Lady-day . . .

and

> shall go thereabouts nightly from two of the clock until they have gone throughout the town. And furthermore they shall be at the demandment of the town during the whole year for further [orders] in their music.

Waits would welcome important visitors, help to celebrate holidays, and take a prominent part in all public ceremonies.

Because of the curious nature of the musical profession, and the particular insecurity experienced by so many musicians during the Renaissance, it was hardly surprising that unions or guilds were established to protect the interests of bona-fide musicians and to exclude the less desirable ones. The musicians of the city of London had before 1500 petitioned successfully for such a guild. A century later, what was in effect a Royal Charter was bestowed upon this 'Company of Musicians'. The political background to such apparently simple

[1] John Stowe, *A Survey of the Cities of London and Westminster*, ed. Strype, Vol. II, p. 2, London, 1608; quoted in a paper given by David Harris to the Royal Musical Association on 27 April 1939, entitled 'Musical Education in Tudor Times'.

[2] There is a chapter entitled 'Cambridge Waits and Orlando Gibbons' in an interesting book by Florence Ada Keynes, *By-Ways of Cambridge History*, 2nd edition, Heffer and Sons Ltd., Cambridge, 1956.

achievements is surprisingly complicated and was evidently of burning anxiety to the musicians of the period. The rapidly growing population of London included musicians of all types and nationalities: royal musicians, household musicians accompanying their patrons on court visits, minstrels, vagabonds, and so on. It is understandable that responsible musicians sought to bring order out of such chaos. Guilds promoted a kind of musical freemasonry, having fraternal, governmental and economic objectives, and they were also much concerned with musical education. Apprenticeships were arranged and new music and ideas exchanged at large-scale meetings.

No doubt the best musical education in the Renaissance, as in any era, was to be gained from personal contact with, and instruction from, one or more of the eminent musicians of the day. From the purist's point of view, a good deal of the energies of such men must have been dissipated in teaching aristocratic pupils, who might or might not display aptitude for music. Those who did, however, would no doubt foster regard for music in high places later on, so that other musicians would ultimately benefit. It would be hard to over-estimate the contribution made by William Byrd, for example, who was not only the outstanding English composer of his day in every field of music but was also an outstanding teacher. Among his pupils were Lady Nevill, for whom he wrote the substantial volume of keyboard music entitled *My Ladye-Nevells Booke*, and the ever-grateful Thomas Morley whom we have already met as author and composer.

EXERCISE

What opportunities existed for the education of musical boys in England during the Renaissance and Reformation period?

SPECIMEN ANSWER

There were a variety of opportunities for the musical and general education of musical boys. Before the dissolution of the monasteries, for example, large numbers of musical boys were employed as singers and in return received a musical and some general education. Such opportunities continued at Oxford, Cambridge and a few exceptional colleges. Some grammar schools made provision for musical instruction. Outstanding education in sacred music was to be had at the Royal Chapels for these employed the best musicians and also had the power to press-gang talented children from cathedrals and churches. Thus a child there would be surrounded by first-rate professionals, and talented contemporaries. The King's Music was a very tight group and education within it was presumably on a personal or family basis. It would necessarily have been of a high order to maintain overall standards and to ensure that sons were fit to follow in their fathers' footsteps. In the country at large, instrumental tuition and instruction in a variety of professional matters were available only to those properly apprenticed. It was of course possible to receive instruction from individuals as an amateur. Oxford and Cambridge Universities also offered theoretical instruction in music as part of the curriculum, and from the latter part of the fifteenth century it was possible to take a musical degree in composition. We include university education among that available to a boy, since some entered university very young. (It was possible to enter as a *sizar*, that is, to have one's education provided in return for performing certain menial duties. Orlando Gibbons, for example, matriculated in the Easter Term of 1598 as a sizar from King's College, Cambridge, at which time he was fifteen.)

Although in this section of the unit we have attempted to show that in Renaissance society music was not such a universally-shared experience as is sometimes thought and that not every household, rich and poor alike, comprised musical connoisseurs who indulged in music-making at the slightest provocation, yet it cannot be denied that by and large music and musicians in Renaissance society enjoyed an esteem and appreciation previously unequalled in the history of music. This regard for music permeated a wider spectrum of society as the sixteenth century progressed, partly because the increasing freedom of religious life and the less exclusive nature of religious art encouraged lay participation and this in turn was furthered by the availability of printed music and musical treatises. In Italy the aristocratic dilettanti founded societies for the promotion of music within their own small but powerful societies – although this was at times hardly necessary since music was already regarded as a natural part of civilized life. We have seen the importance of the gifted amateur and the Italian experimenters, notably the Florentine Camerata.

Finally, nothing is more surprising than the apparent ease and unconcern with which men travelled throughout Europe during the Renaissance. Artists were particularly active in this respect, and it is probably true to say that musicians have never been such an international fraternity as they were in this period. Great numbers of Northern musicians worked in Italy. Indeed, paradoxically, the most eminent composers of the Italian High Renaissance, with the exception of the two most renowned of all, Palestrina and Monteverdi, were mostly Netherlanders: in 1527 Adrian Willaert became *maestro di cappella* of St. Mark's Venice, the most coveted musical post in Italy, and served there for thirty-five years; his first organist and assistant was another Netherlander; Willaert's successor, the almost equally famous Cipriano de Rore (1516–65) was yet another. Two prominent composers of Italian madrigals were Netherlanders, Arcadelt (c. 1505; died after 1567) and Wert (1535–96). Two other outstanding Netherlanders emigrated to central Europe and died there: Orlandus Lassus (via Sicily) and Philip de Monte (via Naples).

There were English singers in Italian establishments – as long ago as during the Wars of the Roses Italian envoys had been sent to England to recruit singers, since they had long been acknowledged as the finest in Europe – and many Italian musicians worked at the English court, especially instrumentalists. There were also distinguished foreign visitors to England, such as the Spanish organist and composer Cabezon, and the well-travelled Philip de Monte, to mention only two.

Flemish and German instrument-makers came to London and set up workshops there. Even paper (for all types of printing) was imported throughout the greater part of the sixteenth century, mainly from France.

Although musicians have always of necessity travelled far and wide, the Renaissance was exceptional in this respect and in the consequent cross-fertilization of ideas and techniques. A central, European musical style evolved as a consequence and remains perhaps the principal musical achievement of the Renaissance. Erasmus, no friend of music, could in fact well have been speaking of music when he uttered his prophetic words 'The world is coming to its senses as if awakening out of a deep sleep'. Nothing could describe more aptly the rich flowering of musical thought, activity, experiment and appreciation, that occurred during the late Renaissance.

SECTION B
RENAISSANCE MUSICAL INSTRUMENTS

Figure 2 Anonymous fifteenth-century painting showing lute, spinet, recorder and bass viol (Bourges Museum).

Among the many foreign musicians working at the English court during the sixteenth century was a Netherlander, Philip van Wilder. There are many references to him in the royal account books, for as well as being employed as lutenist and composer he was 'Keeper of the Instruments to King Henry VIII' – at whose death in 1547 Wilder compiled an inventory of the royal musical instruments listing over three hundred and fifty of them. This large figure includes large numbers of the same sort of instrument – for example, seventy-seven recorders, twenty-eight organs – but, more important, reveals a large variety of different types. Particularly interesting is the predominance of wind instruments over stringed ones, a situation parallelled in an inventory of the Berlin court orchestra made in 1582, and the reverse of the situation which has existed since the nineteenth century.

The names of some of the instruments mentioned in the two inventories are familiar: flutes, organs, bagpipes, guitars, horns, trombones and harp. Others may be unfamiliar: shawms, crumhorns, virginals, perhaps. However we cannot assume that a familiar name denotes a familiar instrument. For example, the Renaissance trombone, while looking more or less like the one we know today, had a narrower bore and a less-flared bell. Its tone was gentler, sweeter, and as suited to playing with 'soft' indoor instruments as with the louder outdoor ones. In England this instrument was called the sackbut.

Today we have two main families of reed instruments, the clarinet family (single reeds) and the oboe family (double reeds). There are several sizes of clarinet of course, and several oboes (cor anglais, bassoon, double-bassoon). Yet the Renaissance music-lover could hear such reed instruments as shawms, curtals, racketts, crumhorns, schreirpfeifen, rauschpfeifen, and others too, all found in a rich variety of shapes and sizes. The shawm (the loud-voiced ancestor of the oboe) came in seven sizes, from two to eight feet in length. The sordun, a cylindrical type of bassoon, had its air-channel bent twice within its body to give it the length required for low pitch without excessive length (it had a

30

muffled, gentle tone as a result); the rackett had its air-channel bent nine times within itself, and the smallest of the five sizes of racketts was only six inches long; it had a marvellous buzzing tone-quality quite unlike any instrument heard today.

We have said earlier that we do not want to treat Renaissance musical instruments exhaustively, for this would be inappropriate to our context. We do, however, want to give you an idea of their richness and variety, and to give you a chance to hear some of them for which good music survives. We will discuss these instruments shortly. First however, let us consider why the Renaissance was so rich in musical instruments.

As you now know, the Renaissance saw for the first time in the history of music the development of instrumental music in its own right. Hitherto instruments had been used primarily and well-nigh exclusively to accompany vocal music and dancing. Such instrumental music as had existed in its own right was largely ceremonial, for large spaces (quite probably for out-of-doors) and as such was designed to create broad effects without any high degree of subtlety or flexibility of expression. Brass instruments like trumpets and trombones in particular were appropriate for such occasions.

The growing secularization of sixteenth-century society meant that music was less frequently confined to church or to the ceremonial occasion. Chamber music became increasingly popular in royal and noble households and later, with the advent of music-printing, it spread to the emergent middle-classes too. In the English noble households it was sometimes provided by a composer-in-residence who might previously have been employed by the church before the Reformation. Chamber music became at the same time more sophisticated in content and presentation. Subtle sounds which would have been lost in a large church or in the open-air were appropriate to the lively acoustic of wood-panelled Renaissance halls. Wooden instruments had a natural affinity to such surroundings and most Renaissance instruments were, in fact, made of wood. Metal (usually brass) was used less than in later periods.

Yet this growing secularization of music during the sixteenth century does not in itself account for the increasing interest in purely instrumental music. It is likely that instruments would have continued to be used primarily to serve vocal music had it not been for the fact that there was, as we have already seen, a change in vocal styles, resulting from the new humanistic literary consciousness. Instead of the music portraying broad, general sentiments, music and poetry were now closely allied in secular music in particular, and individual concepts even individual words, were treated with lively musical imagery. A handful of practised singers (one to a part) around a table would have been able to achieve a remarkably integrated and sensitive performance and it seems likely that they would have preferred to be unfettered by supporting instrumentalists who could not hope to achieve a similar correspondence with the text.

Instrumentalists may sometimes have doubled singers, of course; sometimes they may have alternated with them, substituted for them, or joined in the refrain. Sometimes singers were their own instrumentalists, singing and playing alternately. (Hence, no doubt, the phrase 'apt for voices or viols' mentioned earlier.) Yet the concept of invariable instrumental support, of the instrumentalists' subordination to the singers was weakening, and the natural corollary was a growth of interest in instrumental music in its own right. This was enhanced by the new awareness of harmonic movement, and instruments which could play chords (that is, harmonically) were highly prized. Those that could not do so were made in families to achieve a similar result.

Renaissance polyphony required smooth, blending tone-qualities, not contrasting ones as in the Middle Ages – and this again strengthened the need for large families providing homogeneous tone-colours.

Let us now consider some of the principle musical instruments of the Renaissance. We will divide them into three groups: stringed, wind and keyed.

Stringed Instruments

There were two chief types of Renaissance stringed instruments: the viols, which were bowed consort (ensemble) instruments; and the lute, which was a plucked solo instrument. Viols are often considered as the forerunners of the violin family in the same way that the lute is considered the forerunner of the guitar, and the harpsichord the forerunner of the piano. This is true only in the loose sense that there is a superficial resemblence between each type and its 'successor', and that viol music is quite often performed on violins in the absence of viols, just as the guitar or piano are used in default of a lute or harpsichord. Yet viols and violins existed side by side in the Renaissance and only in the seventeenth century did the violin family oust the viols, very largely because they were better suited to playing the new, brilliant and highly expressive Italian music of the early Baroque era – music which soon dominated European musical taste. The less flexible, gentler viols, with their characteristic nasal tone, although ideal for Renaissance polyphony in which each part was of more or less equal importance, could not adapt to the new musical style and so fell into disuse. Only the bass viol survived, being used well into the eighteenth century as a 'continuo' instrument. (The 'continuo' or 'continuous support' was necessary in Baroque compositions and usually comprised at least one harmonic instrument such as the harpsichord, organ, or lute, together with a stringed bass instrument.)

The viols family had three principal members: treble, tenor and bass. There was also a double bass viol. Each instrument had six strings and was fretted. (Frets are loops of catgut on the neck marking off semitonal divisions.) Members of the violin family – violin, viola, cello – then as now had four strings, although the double-bass, which since the nineteenth century has had four or five strings, previously had either three or four. The violin family is unfretted. Viols have flat backs, violins rounded ones; viols are bowed differently from violins and furthermore, the treble and tenor viols are held upright on the knee when being played (hence the family is called *viole de gamba* since *gamba* is the Italian word for leg). Viols, like lutes and harpsichords, are made and played again today, owing to the revival of interest in early music and the desire to hear it on the instrument for which it was composed.

The lute, as we have said, was the Renaissance instrument *par excellence*. It was portable, exceedingly expressive, the ideal instrument for accompanying a singer, yet capable of performing surprisingly complex solo polyphony; it could also provide its own melody (with virtuosic embellishments) and simultaneous accompaniment. Over two thousand pieces of lute music survive in England alone (over three times the number of surviving keyboard pieces), adequate testimony to the regard in which the instrument was held. The sixteenth-century lute had five 'courses' (ten actual strings, arranged in pairs) and a sixth course was usual by around 1600. The lute, like the viol, was fretted. Further courses were soon added and longer strings called 'diapasons' ran from a second neck.

During the Renaissance larger types of lute were constructed: the theorbo or arch-lute with extra gut diapason strings and the nasal-sounding chitarrone with wire strings.

Figure 3 Vittore Carpaccio: Child playing a Lute: detail from Presentazione al Sacerdote Simeon. *Venice Academy (Mansell Collection).*

The lute has a pear-shaped body with rounded back, whereas the guitar is shaped something like a figure eight and has a flat back. The cittern family lies halfway between the two: rounded sides like the lute, but with a flat back like the guitar. The cittern's strings (four to twelve pairs) are usually of wire. A pandora or bandora is a type of large-scale cittern.

Wind Instruments

There were two main families of flute: the transverse flute, keyless, cylindrical and the ancestor of our modern orchestral flute; and the recorder or fipple flute played straight from the lips as with other wind instruments. The leading group was the recorders, which were found in up to nine or ten sizes. The recorder is a simple wooden pipe, tapering slightly inwards towards the lower end, almost stopped at the top by a wooden plug, but with a narrow flue which allows the player's breath to pass and strike against a sharp edge of a mouthhole in the top-side of the pipe, as with a whistle. The effective length of pipe can be shortened and the pitch it provides varied by the player opening holes in it with his fingers. The recorder's tone is smooth, sweet, and clear, well-suited again to Renaissance polyphony. Indeed, there is an old-English verb 'to record' meaning 'to warble' (like a bird), and it is from this that the word recorder derives.

Shawms, already mentioned, were double-reed wind instruments, as are the modern oboe and bassoon. However, the shawm's reed was taken right inside the player's mouth, whereas the oboe reed is held between the player's lips. Some shawms were so large that it was not possible to reach the lower holes with the fingers, and a key or lever-mechanism was adopted to solve the problem. There was even a gross-bass pommer ten-foot long. The rauschpfeife (or schreirpfeife) was another type of shawm.

Figure 4 Vittore Carpaccio. Girl playing a crumhorn: detail from Presentazione al Sacerdote Simeone. Venice Academy (Mansell Collection).

One of the most important inventions of the sixteenth century was the proto-type of the modern bassoon: the curtal or dulcian. By doubling the conical tube back on itself makers achieved a great technical advance over the larger and more cumbersome types of shawm. Although the bass or 'double' curtal was destined to become the most important member of the family, there were several other sizes from 'soprano' to 'great bass'. The double-tube idea was obviously considered a success and was tried out on other instruments: the sordun or courtaut (two cylindrical tubes) and the rackett (eight or nine cylindrical tubes).

Some double-reed instruments had the reeds enclosed in a wooden chamber, the player activating them by blowing through a narrow slit. The most widely used was the crumhorn ('curved horn') a curious-looking instrument with conical bore and the usual small fingerholes. Difficult to play, it had a uniform and rather penetrating tone-quality. (Many of these Renaissance instruments are found in a variety of English spellings, by the way; we have adopted the more usual 'modern' spellings and have not thought it advisable to add to the confusion by giving foreign equivalents – which have their own variants.)

Whereas in the above wind instruments the sound is initiated by the double-reed – actually pieces of cane mounted to beat against one another – there is a type of instrument in which this function is provided by the human lips,

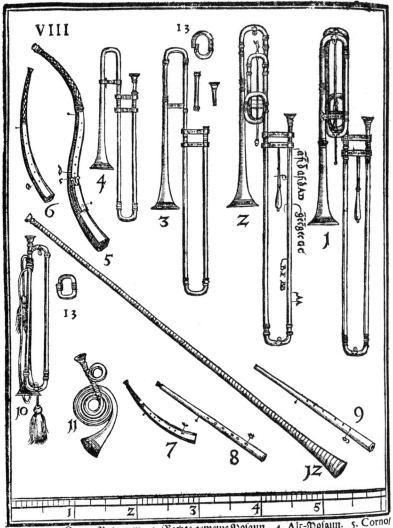

1. 2. Quart-Poſaunen. 3. Rechte gemeine Poſaun. 4. Alt-Poſaunn. 5. Cornoſ Groß Tenor-Cornet. 6. Recht Chor-Zinck. 7. Klein Diſcant-Zinck / ſo ein Quint höher. 8. Gerader Zinck mit ein Mundſtück. 9. Still-Zinck. 10. Trommet. 11. Jäger-Trommet. 12. Hölzern Trommet. 13. Krumbbügel auff ein gantz Thon.

Figure 5 A plate from the second volume (1619) of Syntagma Musicum (1615–20) *by Michael Praetorius showing trombones (Nos. 1–4), cornetts (No. 5, tenor; Nos. 6–7, curved; Nos. 8–9, straight), trumpets (Nos. 10–12) and crooks (No. 13), extra tubing which enables a player to lower the fundamental note of the instrument. The scale at the bottom of the plate relates to the 'Brunswick Yard' (=English Yard). Each major division – 1, 2, 3, etc. – represents ¼ yard or nine inches (Cambridge University Library).*

which are pressed against a cup or mouthpiece. The archetype is the trumpet, an instrument which dates back to antiquity. In the sixteenth century, however, there was an extremely popular type of *wooden* instrument (as opposed to metal, invariably used for trumpets and trombones) called the cornett or zink, which nevertheless used the lip-principle of the trumpet family. Cornetts provided a kind of in-between stage between woodwind and brass families and were especially popular because of the guild rules which restricted trumpet playing to certain privileged members. Cornetts could be straight, curved, or in the case of the tenor cornett, shaped like a letter S. The largest bass member, developed in the seventeenth century, was the serpent and this was shaped like a double S.

Trumpets and trombones in the sixteenth century mostly resembled modern ones, although the trumpet had no valves. Some trumpets, however, were ornately formed, but both the trumpets and trombones had smaller bells and narrower bores, giving a softer tone than their present-day counterparts. This, as we have already noted, allowed them to take part more readily in chamber-music ensembles. There were two types of trumpeter, by the way: the *Feldtrompeter* or field-trumpeter, who was not expected to read music, and who played simple passages on lower notes; and the *Kammertrompeter* or chamber trumpeter who played the highest notes possible on the 'natural' instruments, the ones where the notes of the harmonic series were sufficiently close together to provide a scalic series. Each class of trumpeter was forbidden by the guild to play in the register of the other. This tradition was alive in Bach's day and accounts for the extremely difficult high trumpet part found in the Second Brandenburg Concerto, for example, which present-day players find so formidable. Players continually used to playing in such a high and difficult register would find Bach's parts practicable.

Keyboard String Instruments

There were two basic types, stringed and wind. The stringed family comprised the clavichord and the harpsichord, with its near relations the virginals and spinet. The only keyed wind instrument is the organ, but that existed in three basic forms, portative, positive, and church organ. The portative was small and as its name suggests, portable, the positive less so, and the church organ could be very large indeed. One other keyed instrument should be mentioned – the regal, a little portative reed-pipe organ.

We have described the clavichord, harpsichord and organ at some length in the Arts Foundation Course, Units 13–14, *Introduction to Music*,[1] where there are also drawings of these instruments. Here is a briefer description.

The clavichord is a very simple keyed instrument. An oblong box contains strings running at right angles to a small keyboard, and these strings are activated by a brass 'tangent' which protrudes from the far end of each key and which also determines its vibrating length. By varying the pressure on the key with the finger, a vibrato can be obtained – that is a small variation of pitch above and below the principal note, of the sort associated with singers, wind players and violinists, but foreign to all other keyboard instruments.

The harpsichord belongs to a family of plucked stringed keyboard instruments. The player's finger depresses a key which activates a rod or jack with a protruding plectrum at the top of it. This plucks the string as it ascends, but is

[1] The Open University (1971) A100 Humanities: A Foundation Course, Units 13–14 *Introduction to Music*, The Open University Press.

allowed to fall back silently by a simple spring mechanism. A damper is attached
to each jack to prevent the string from sounding after the key is released. The
tone of the harpsichord is clear, incisive, yet even – ideal, in fact, for the performance of polyphony. Since the tone of any individual note cannot be
modified (a characteristic of many Renaissance instruments – those having
the reed enclosed in a wooden chamber, for example) makers frequently
provided several sets of strings which could yield differing tonal qualities.
These could be used separately or together, and in a harpsichord with two
keyboards they could be used in contrast too.

Whereas the harpsichord's strings run in the same direction as the keys (as
with a grand piano) the virginals' run at right angles. Although generally
a one-manual instrument, some virginals had a second keyboard to one side
of the principal one, activating a set of strings sounding an octave higher.

*Figure 6 Two-manual harpsi-
chord by Ruckers of Antwerp,
1612 (Musée Instrumentale,
Conservatoire Royal de
Musique de Bruxelles).*

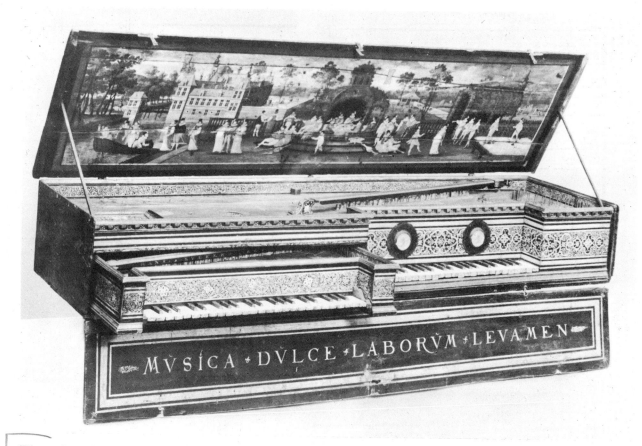

The spinet is properly an Italian virginals, but the term is used (somewhat loosely) to denote any small harpsichord, especially if triangular or leg-of-mutton shaped.

Figure 7 Ruckers Virginals of 1581. The motto means: 'Music is a delightful respite from work' (Metropolitan Museum of Art, New York).

Keyboard Wind Instruments

The portative organ was played with one hand while pumped with the other to provide wind for its tiny bellows. Because one-handed playing could hardly make the most of the new harmonic style, this instrument became less used in the Renaissance.

The positive organ was pumped by a second person leaving the first free to play with both hands. Several ranks of pipes were often provided and such an instrument could be used to accompany voices or viols, for example, or used as a solo instrument.

The regal was a tiny portative organ with reed pipes whose short length did no more than slightly enhance the tuning of the reeds themselves. From the mid-sixteenth century the instrument had a detachable folding keyboard which could be packed up with the bellows. The folded instrument strongly resembled a bible: hence 'Bible Regal'.

The church organ grew in size in the sixteenth century, and its range was considerably augmented by the use of ranks of pipes extending from thirty-two foot pitch to one foot or less. Many varieties of flue and reed pipes were used, also 'mutations' or 'mixtures' – artificial harmonics added to give added brilliance. The organ developed rapidly, particularly in Germany (perhaps because of the ease with which rich keyboard polyphony, much admired by the Germans, could be played on it) and many instruments had several keyboards and a pedal keyboard played by the player's feet.

Figure 9 Strasbourg Cathedral Organ, c. 1490 (Mansell Collection).

Figure 8 A plate from Michael Praetorius' Syntagma Musicum *showing positive organ (No. 1) and regal (No. 2) (Cambridge University Library).*

(The console of such an instrument is normally placed behind the 'positive division', i.e. concealed by the lower case of pipes, to which the player has his back.)

It is not unusual for organs, especially large ones in important buildings, to be rebuilt a number of times. Very often some pipework from earlier instruments is incorporated into later ones. Thus although Strasbourg Cathedral has had several distinct organs – an early one of 1260 being destroyed by fire, as was its successor in 1298 and a third in 1384 – it is not unrealistic to regard the subsequent organs dating from 1385 to 1934 as a single instrument whose character changed according to prevailing fashion. For example, the magnificent organ of *c.* 1490 by Krebs incorporated earlier pipework; this instrument was enlarged, repaired, reconstructed and restored during the following century. In the early eighteenth century it was rebuilt and its character changed by the outstanding builder Andreas Silbermann who, under pressure from the cathedral administration, preserved Krebs' magnificent casework (which you can see in the illustration). Silbermann's classical masterpiece remained virtually unchanged for a hundred and fifty years, but was then transformed into a Romantic 'orchestral' instrument of the kind fashionable in the later years of the nineteenth century. As far as possible, however, Silbermann's ideals were followed in a new instrument of 1834, and some of his pipework which had escaped the nineteenth-century rebuilding was incorporated in it. (We found much of this information in *Les Orgues et les organistes de la cathédrale de Strasbourg* by Félix Raugel published by Editions Alsatia Colmar, 1948.)

SECTION C
RENAISSANCE MUSICAL FORMS

It is convenient when discussing musical forms to divide them into sacred and secular, vocal and instrumental. We do not want to give an exhaustive list of Renaissance musical forms any more than we wanted to list all Renaissance instruments. To do so would blur rather than clarify the picture of Renaissance music and musical life that we are hoping to portray in this unit, and would not necessarily enhance your feeling for the music that you hear in the next two units. Yet too many references to the Mass, the madrigal, the pavan and galliard, and so on, necessarily occur in any discussion of music of this period for us to ignore the subject altogether.

Sacred Vocal Forms

No other single phenomenon has influenced Western musicians as much as the Mass, the central liturgical office of the Roman Catholic Church. The Mass represents the commemoration and mystical re-enactment of the sacrifice of Christ on the cross. For over fifteen hundred years parts of the Mass have been set to music; yet many would agree that the music written for the Mass during the late Renaissance excelled that of any other period in its purity, beauty, and sheer fitness of expression.

The Mass comprises two elements: the Proper, whose texts change from day to day; and the Ordinary, which is invariable. Certain – relatively small – parts of the Mass are set to music and these comprise the 'musical' Mass. Whereas parts of the Proper have been set to countless plainsong chants, composers of polyphonic music (since the fourteenth century) have set the five traditional chants of the Ordinary. These are:

Kyrie Eleison	(=Lord, have mercy)
Gloria in Excelsis	(=Glory be to God on high)
Credo	(=I believe in God)
Sanctus	(=Holy, Holy, Holy)
Agnus Dei	(=Lamb of God)

When we speak of a 'Palestrina Mass' therefore, we mean a setting by him of the Latin texts whose opening words are given above. We examine the Mass *Aeterna Christi munera* (The eternal gifts of Christ) by Palestrina in Unit 18.

Another form, the motet, reached perfection in the Renaissance in the hands of Palestrina, Lassus, Victoria, and Byrd – Italian, Netherlander, Spaniard and Englishman respectively, as we noted previously. A motet is a sacred vocal composition to a Latin text other than from the Mass. It has long been thought to have been performed *a capella* or unaccompanied, although there is some evidence to the contrary. The motet had a long history, flourishing from about 1250–1750 (there are early secular motets, polytextual motets and other special types); there are later motets too – indeed, composers still write them. In Unit 18 we examine William Byrd's motet *Ave verum corpus* (Hail, true body). In the latter part of the sixteenth century, English composers began setting music to vernacular texts and the resulting 'English motet' was called the anthem. The composer followed his own choice of source, but naturally choir-masters took care to ensure that any particular anthem fitted the occasion. An anthem for full choir is called a full anthem, but if soloists are used it is called a verse anthem. Soloists needed instrumental support, so verse anthems are accompanied; in fact, full anthems were probably accompanied too, judging from the evidence of the organ scores which survive.

The Book of Common Prayer specified three 'Services': Matins or Mattins (Morning Service), Evensong, and Communion. This last is the English equivalent of the Roman Mass, but never achieved the overriding importance the Mass enjoyed in the Catholic liturgy.

The parts of the morning service which are often set by composers include the *Venite* ('O come let us sing unto the Lord', psalm 95 according to the English numbering); *Te Deum* ('We praise thee O God', a hymn of praise dating from *c.* 400) and the *Benedictus* ('Blessed be the Lord', a scriptural and liturgical salutation). The two chief songs or 'canticles' set to music in the Evening Service are the *Magnificat* ('My Soul doth magnify the Lord', the song of the Virgin Mary) and the *Nunc Dimittis* ('Now lettest thou thy Servant depart in peace', the song of Simeon). The Communion (or English Mass) portions that composers set to music were generally the same as those in the Roman Mass.

Secular Vocal Forms

One secular vocal form which achieved great popularity during the second half of the sixteenth century was the madrigal. It originated in Italy and developed there under Marenzio (*c.* 1553–1599), Gesualdo (*c.* 1560–1613) and Monteverdi (1567–1643) into a dramatic idiom which paved the way for the rise of opera in the early seventeenth century. It crossed the Alps and reached England shortly after the middle of the sixteenth century, but it was not until the celebrated publication *Musica Transalpina* appeared in 1588 that the English madrigal flowered in the hands of men like Byrd (1543–1623), Morley (1557?–1603?), Weelkes (?–1623) and Wilbye (1574–1638). (*Musica Transalpina* was a collection of Italian madrigals provided with English texts and published by Nicholas Yonge.)

Early madrigals were more chordal than later ones, and were likely to be rather gentle settings of pastoral poetry. Middle-period madrigals are more contrapuntal (the various 'voices' or 'parts' weave in a more linear fashion) and the spirit of the text becomes more closely reflected in the music. Whereas the early madrigals had often been written for four voices, the middle-period ones were usually for five or six. Love-poetry was favoured. The late Italian madrigal became altogether more highly charged, emotionally and musically; experimental harmony, virtuosic solos, the highest order of word-painting, all combined to lead away from the balanced art of the Renaissance into the extravagance of the Baroque. In Unit 18 we shall consider one Italian madrigal, *Baci soavi e cari* (Kisses, tender and dear) by Monteverdi, and two English pieces, one by Thomas Morley and the other by Orlando Gibbons.

There were some German and Spanish madrigals, but the French preferred the chanson or polyphonic song. This was contrapuntal, involving systematic imitation, and showed a particular sensitivity to correct accentuation. Jannequin (*c.* 1485–*c.* 1564) was one of the chief composers of the sixteenth-century French chanson. Many of his chansons were published in his lifetime by Attaingnant, and were programmatic: for example, 'The Cries of Paris', 'The Song of the Birds', 'The Hunt', and so on.

A favourite secular vocal form particularly in England, was the lute-song, ayre, or air, a generally short and expressive piece for voice and lute. Composer and poet might be one: likewise singer and accompanist. Lute-songs were usually strophic, that is, having the same music for each verse of the text. Some however, such as the very moving *In darkness let me dwell* by John Dowland (1562–1626), are 'through-composed', that is, the music unfolds as the text proceeds, without strophic repetition. Other English lute-song composers of the period include Thomas Morley (1558–1603), Philip Rosseter (*c.* 1575–1623), Thomas Campian (1567–1620), and Robert Jones (dates of birth and death unknown); John Cooper (d. 1626) – or Cop(e)rario as he was known after his supposed Italian sojourn – is interesting in that his lute-songs show some influence of the Florentine Camerata. He appears to have been the first Englishman to write monody.[1] We shall hear three lute-songs by Dowland, – including *In darkness let me dwell* – in the radio programme on the lute-song.

EXERCISE

(Relating to sacred and secular vocal forms.)

Match up the following terms with their definitions:

1	Mass	An English motet, written in the vernacular.	(a)
2	Motet	Matins, Evensong, or Communion.	(b)
3	Anthem	Central liturgical office of the Roman Catholic Church.	(c)
4	Madrigal	Sacred vocal composition to a Latin text other than from Ordinary of the Mass.	(d)
5	Chanson	Vocal composition of Italian origin with secular words.	(e)
6	English Service	Polyphonic song, more contrapuntal than the madrigal.	(f)

ANSWER

1 c
2 d
3 a
4 e
5 f
6 b

Instrumental Forms

Turning to instrumental music, we can discern two main types: one derived from vocal music; the other, dance music. Within these two categories a number of specific forms are discovered.

[1] See the preface to *The English Lute-Songs*, First Series 17, *John Coprario: Funeral Teares (1606), Songs of Mourning (1613), The Masque of Squires (1614)*, transcribed and edited by Gerald Hendrie and Thurston Dart, London, Stainer and Bell Ltd., 1959.

The most obvious example of the first type is the instrumental arrangement of a favourite madrigal or chanson. Such arrangements could be for a solo instrument or for an ensemble or 'consort'. Thus the lovely 5-part chanson *Faulte d'argent* (Lack of money is the worst of evils) by the outstanding Netherlands composer Josquin des Près (1450–1521) turns up a century later arranged for organ and therefore quite probably used in a sacred context, by the Italian Girolamo Cavazzoni (b. *c.* 1515).

Plainsongs, the chants of the Catholic church, also form the backbone of many instrumental works. The chant moves in slow notes in one part while the other parts weave counterpoints around it. Clearly this is well-suited to viols or keyboard compositions.

Variations on popular songs were an especial delight of the English virginals composers or 'virginalists', and although these songs were folksongs (in the sense that they were not specifically composed together with accompaniments by identifiable composers but 'grew up' of their own accord) we can nevertheless validly consider such instrumental variations to have been vocally-inspired. There were many first-rate English Renaissance songs, and as Willi Apel rightly observes in the fourth volume of *The New Oxford History of Music* 'No other country can boast such a wealth of charming popular sixteenth-century melodies, no other country a group of composers who, recognizing the value of this treasure, cultivated and enhance it.' Here are several of these tunes, each of which we have given at a pitch suitable for playing on the recorder:

1 Up Tails All

2 The Woods So Wilde

3 Come John, Kiss Me Now

4   O Mistress Mine

5   Walsingham

6   Go From My Window

Dance-music was frequently improvised over one of several standard basses in much the same way that jazz or pop musicians work today. Indeed, the best-loved of all Renaissance 'grounds' was the Passymeasures or Passamezzo whose bass and fundamental harmonies are those of the twelve-bar blues. Yet much dance-music was notated and among such notated forms we find especially the pavan and galliard, two staple dances often set as a pair, in contrasting rhythm and tempo: the pavan, slow and stately in four beats to the bar (or 'common time'); the galliard, lively and more energetic in three beats to the bar. But just as the Chopin waltz of the nineteenth century was no longer designed to be danced to, so the stylized pavans and galliards of the late Renaissance, often surprisingly irregular in construction, were clearly intended as art-music. Both pavan and galliard were normally in three sections, by the way, each with varied repeats, sometimes improvised, sometimes notated.

An instrumental form of particular significance is the fantasia, or fancy, as the English often called it. This was a piece where various short phrases were treated imitatively (in 'points' of imitation) that is, echoed by successive parts and developed. The texture frequently overlaps, with all the richness and restrained profusion of true Renaissance art. As Thomas Morley wrote, in his *A Plain and Easy Introduction to Practical Music* of 1597:

> The most principal and chiefest kind of music which is made without a ditty [i.e. freely-composed] is the Fantasy, that is when a musician taketh a point at his pleasure and wresteth and turneth it as he list, making either much or little of it according as shall seem best in his own conceit.

The fantasy was the forerunner of the fugue of Bach's day, but whereas Bach's fugues were often preceded by an introduction or 'prelude', the Renaissance prelude seems to have existed as a piece in its own right. There were two types of prelude: the slow solemn prelude, used to precede a vocal composition in church; and the brilliant, dashing prelude designed to show off a player's finger-skill or 'touch'. The second sort were called 'toccatas' from the Italian *toccare*, to touch. We examine a brilliant prelude by Orlando Gibbons in Unit 19.

Finally there are loosely descriptive pieces with fanciful titles such as 'The Fall of the Leaf', 'Tower Hill', 'The Earl of Oxford's March'; and others such as 'Mr. Byrd's Battle', 'The Bells', 'Giles Farnaby's Dream' which are early examples of programme music – to give just a few examples of English pieces that fall into these two categories. These pieces are often miniatures and the descriptive element may seem to us to border on the naive. Yet simplicity is no fault and the poetry of 'Giles Farnaby's Dream' (another piece we shall examine in Unit 19) is no less moving for being contained within such a fleeting moment of time.

UNIT 18   RENAISSANCE MUSIC PART II

Introduction

There is a vast amount of surviving Renaissance vocal music and it was far from easy to decide what pieces to discuss in this unit. We have limited the selection to Italian and English music, regretfully ignoring the splendid music of the Netherlands and Spain. We deal with the sacred pieces first, and then with the secular: thus the Italian and English music of each type is juxtaposed. The unit accompanies side one of the gramophone record.

As an example of Italian sacred music we shall consider a late work by Giovanni Pierluigi da Palestrina (c. 1525–94), the Mass *Aeterna Christi munera* (The eternal gifts of Christ) of 1590; and of English sacred music, the short motet by William Byrd (1543–1623) *Ave verum corpus* (Hail, true body) which was published in 1605. Again, this is a later work, but seems to us to represent the quintessence of Byrd's vocal style, just as the *Aeterna Christi munera* work represents the quintessence of Palestrina's vocal style. Together they fairly represent the culmination of Renaissance sacred polyphony in the hands of two of the outstanding composers of that period.

As examples of Italian secular music we shall consider the madrigal *Baci soavi e cari* (Kisses, tender and dear) by Claudio Monteverdi (1567–1643). Monteverdi composed eight books of madrigals, published between 1587 and 1638, and a ninth was published posthumously. Broadly speaking, the first four are in the late Renaissance style and the remainder in the early Baroque style. *Baci soavi e cari* is found in Book I. English secular vocal music is represented by the madrigal *April is in my mistress' face* of 1594 by Thomas Morley (1558–1603) and the part-song *The silver swan* of 1612 by Orlando Gibbons (1583–1625). All the above composers, by the way, are known generally by their surnames only – Palestrina, Byrd, Monteverdi, Morley – with the exception of Orlando Gibbons whose Christian name is necessary to distinguish him from his musical father, brothers, and particularly his son Christopher.

Thus we shall study five pieces of late Renaissance music altogether: an Italian Mass and English motet; an Italian madrigal, an English madrigal, and an English part-song.

EXERCISE

The Byrd motet should seem to you somewhat exceptional in view of what you have read about Renaissance musical forms in Unit 17. Why?

SPECIMEN ANSWER

Ave verum corpus is exceptional because it was published in 1605, a considerable while after most English composers began setting sacred texts in the vernacular.

DISCUSSION

Although the Catholic faith was still practised discreetly in parts of England in Elizabethan and Jacobean England and music was no doubt used at celebrations of the various Offices, it is astonishing that a composer could actually have published a Latin motet at such a date. Byrd, however, published two sets of motets for liturgical use in the early years of the seventeenth century under the title of *Gradualia* (Graduals) of 1605 and 1607. He also composed and had published three Masses, for three, four, and five voices respectively. The date of publication of the Masses is not known since the surviving printed copies bear no title page: Fellowes, in *William Byrd*, suggests that no music publisher would have risked publishing the Masses under their true title at this time and that they were published discreetly, perhaps even in conjunction with the first book of *Gradualia* of 1605. As we have noted in Unit 17, Byrd remained a Catholic all his life, yet retained his position as a Gentleman of the Chapel Royal from his appointment there in 1570 until his death more than fifty years later – not without some problems resulting from his faith, but without serious molestation. He wrote music for both the Catholic and the Reformed Anglican Church with equal conviction and sincerity. He was acknowledged the greatest musician of his day and this no doubt played its part in his somewhat anomalous position at the courts of Elizabeth and James I.

(We have chosen Byrd's *Ave verum corpus* in preference to an English anthem such as Orlando Gibbons' verse anthem *This is the record of John*, because we wished to give examples of the two chief sacred forms, Mass and Motet; and also because Byrd's piece, though short and straightforward, represents the culmination of the English polyphonic style of the late Renaissance whether used in conjunction with Latin or with English words.)

Incidentally, if you already know Orlando Gibbons' *The silver swan* you might have considered this exceptional, for it is by no means a typical madrigal, being more of a pensive, moralistic, part-song. Yet Gibbons himself included it as the first piece in his *First Set of Madrigals and Motets of Five Parts* – a curious title, in fact, since all the texts are English ones, and furthermore he made no attempt to indicate which he considered to be madrigals and which motets. However, Gibbons' music is mostly characterized by a seriousness of purpose and somewhat taut, even nervous, manner, and so quite possibly he regarded the seriousness of some of the poems he set in his *First Book* as being worthy of the term motet. Regarding his use of the term 'madrigal', we shall discuss this when examining *The silver swan*.

1   Missa: Aeterna Christi munera (Mass: The eternal gifts of Christ) by Giovanni Pierluigi da Palestrina (*c.* 1525–94)

Giovanni Pierluigi was born at Palestrina (the ancient Praeneste) about twenty miles south-east of Rome. He later added the name of his birthplace to his own – a not uncommon procedure – and became known as Palestrina. He never travelled outside the small triangle of Palestrina, Rome and Tivoli (about fifteen miles east of Rome) but made a series of rather complicated moves within it. He went to Rome as a chorister and studied music there. In 1544 he returned to Palestrina to take charge of music at the cathedral. His local bishop was later to become Pope Julius III and perhaps a high regard for the composer explains why Julius called him to Rome a few years later to become choirmaster of the Julian Chapel of St Peter's. Palestrina's first book of Masses of 1554 is dedicated to Julius III, who appointed him a singer in the

Pontifical Choir in January of the following year. In addition to singing, Palestrina acted as composer to the Papal Chapel. He gave up his old appointment in the Julian Chapel.

Figure 10 Palestrina presenting his Masses to the Pope (From a 'curious print from wood or metal after the design of some great painter' which appears in a 1572 publication of his Masses. Source: John Hawkins, A General History of the Science and Practice of Music, London 1776, modern reprint, Dover Publications, Inc., New York, 1963).

At this point in his life the good fortune and recognition that Palestrina had so far enjoyed began to desert him. Julius died in March 1555. His successor, Marcellus II, died after only three weeks as Pope, but had initiated reforms unfavourable to Palestrina and which were continued by the following Pope, Paul IV. (These reforms will be mentioned again in Units 26–27, *The Catholic Reformation*.) Amongst other things, married singers were to be excluded from the choir. Palestrina had married in 1547, so with two other married colleagues he was dismissed with a small pension. For the next five years, until 1560, Palestrina was choirmaster at St John Lateran, Rome (a post vacated by the outstanding Netherlander, Orlando di Lasso) but conditions were not satisfactory. He next took charge of the music of the Cappella Liberiana at Santa

Maria Maggiore (St Mary the Greater) Rome, the chapel in which he had been a choirboy, and for a few months also took charge of some concerts in Tivoli where his patron-Cardinal had a villa, the Villa d'Este.

Around 1566 he became the first director of music at a newly-established Roman Seminary. Then he returned to the Villa d'Este, but soon considered moving to Vienna to become director of music at the court of the Emperor Maximillian II. His interest in the post was taken seriously but the salary he demanded was too high. The composer Philip de Monte was appointed instead in 1568. In the same year Palestrina began a fruitful association with Duke Gonzaga of Mantua. This lasted five years, after which Palestrina returned to his old post of director of music at the Julian Chapel. He remained there until his death.

Palestrina's output is large, though nearly all in the field of sacred vocal music. There are over a hundred surviving Masses, two hundred and fifty motets, thirteen complete sets of the Lamentations of Jeremiah, and about two hundred other sacred pieces. There were also some madrigals, both sacred and secular. His complete works comprise over thirty volumes in the modern edition.

What made this man's music so remarkable? Why, for several hundred years, have countless music students been given his music to study and to re-work? Why, even in the 1970s, are examination papers set on 'Palestrinian counterpoint' in many universities? In the eighteenth century, Sir John Hawkins wrote that Palestrina

> sedulously applied himself to the study of harmony, and by the use of such combinations as naturally suggest themselves to a nice and unprejudiced ear, formed a style so simple, so pathetic, and withal so sublime, that his compositions for the church are even at this day looked on as the models of harmonical perfection.[1]

Seventy years or so later, the composer Robert Schumann (1810–56) wrote of Palestrina and his music in a letter to F. Brendel dated 3 July 1848 that

> At times it really sounds like the music of the spheres, and then, what art! I really believe he is the greatest muscial genius Italy has ever produced.

A striking tribute was paid by another nineteenth-century composer, Charles Gounod (1818–93), best known today for the ballet music to his opera *Faust* and for some delightful songs. As a student at the Paris Conservatoire he won the coveted Rome Prize for composition and while in Rome he studied Renaissance sacred music. In his *Memoirs*[2] he recalls the powerful effect that hearing Palestrina's music in the Sistine Chapel of St Peter's, with its ceiling painted by Michelangelo, had on him:

> There are works that must be seen or heard in the places for which they were created. The Sistine Chapel is one of these exceptional places, unique of its kind in the world. The colossal genius who decorated its vaulted ceiling and the wall of the altar with his matchless conceptions of the story of Genesis and of the Last Judgment, the painter of the prophets, with whom he seemed to be on an equality, will, doubtless, never have his equal, no more than Homer or Phidias. Men of this stamp and stature are not seen twice upon the earth; they are syntheses, they embrace a whole world, they exhaust it, they complete it, and what they have said no one can repeat after them. The music of Palestrina seems to be a translation in song of the vast poem of Michael Angelo, [Michelangelo] and I am inclined to think that these two masters explain and illustrate each other in the same light, the spectator developing the listener, and reciprocally, so that, finally, one is tempted to ask if the Sistine Chapel – painting and music – is not the product of one and the same inspiration . . .

[1] *Op. cit.*, Vol. 1, p. 390 of modern edition.
[2] *Mémoires d'un artiste*, posthumous, 1896.

There are in fact, between the works of Michael Angelo and of Palestrina such analogies, such a similarity of ideas, that it is very difficult not to conclude that these two privileged beings were possessed of the same combination of qualities, and I was about to say, of virtues. In both the same simplicity, the same modesty in the employment of means, the same indifference to effect, the same disdain of seductive attractions. One feels that the material agent, the hand, counts for nothing, and that the soul alone, unalterably fixed upon a higher world, strives only to express in a humble and subordinate form the sublimity of its contemplations.

Figure 11 Interior of the Sistine Chapel (Mansell Collection).

Two modern historians of music, Donald Grout and Gustave Reese, show a more objective and scholarly attitude to Palestrina – but their conclusions are nevertheless much the same as those of Hawkins, Schumann and Gounod, and of numerous other musicians past and present. Grout in *A History of Western Music* writes (p. 239)

No other composer before Bach is so well known by name as Palestrina, and no other composer's technique has been subject to more scrutiny. He has been called the 'Prince of Music' and his works the 'absolute perfection' of church style. It is generally recognized that, better than any other composer, he captured the essence of the sober, conservative aspect of the Counter Reformation in a polyphony of utter purity, completely detached from any secular suggestion. The Palestrina style is exemplified most clearly in his Masses; its objective, coolly impersonal quality is most appropriate to the formal and ritualistic texts of the Ordinary.

A few years earlier, in *Music in the Renaissance*, Gustave Reese had written (p. 459)

> The position of Palestrina in the history of music is in some ways anomalous. His sacred works have long been regarded as representing the ideal application of polyphony to music for the Catholic Church. Nevertheless, a slightly derogatory attitude has taken form in some quarters during the 20th century, as a reaction against romanticization of the composer in the 19th century, when he was looked upon as a lonely figure without a flaw. The more recent view has replaced overvaluation with undervaluation. Actually, Palestrina, in his church music, reveals himself as one of the three greatest composers of the twilight period in Renaissance music, the other two being Lassus and Byrd[1] . . . The spiritual quality of Palestrina's sacred compositions, even when they are based on secular prototypes, is not to be denied[2]; his technical proficiency is such as to make the old legend of flawlessness almost credible.

Rather than attempt a further verbal explanation of Palestrina's outstanding position in the history of music, we hope that his music itself will persuade you that the above opinions are valid. If our discussion of *Aeterna Christi munera* helps you in this, we shall be pleased; but if you took the Arts Foundation Course you will remember that we believe that however much we talk about music, music remains music and must be judged in musical terms. As Mendelssohn once remarked, 'the thoughts expressed by music are not too vague for words but too precise' – and if he was right, then no amount of discussion can act as a substitute for actual musical experience. We can perhaps open doors, but it is you who must walk through them.

Figure 12 Palestrina (Radio Times Hulton Picture Library).

The Mass *Aeterna Christi munera*, dedicated on 1 June 1590 to William V of Bavaria, is one of Palestrina's later works. Yet in his last years Palestrina, like many other composers, was able to achieve some of his finest results with simpler means than he might have employed previously. Thus all the movements of *Aeterna Christi munera* except the final one are for only four voices (soprano, alto, tenor, bass) – whereas a number of earlier Masses had been for

---

[1] We would add a fourth. Do you remember who?

[2] Renaissance Masses and motets were sometimes based on secular musical material.

five or six voices. *Aeterna Christi munera* is also a relatively short and straight-forward piece, showing great restraint and serenity.

There were five main types of Mass-settings in the sixteenth century, four of them based on pre-existing musical material and the fifth freely-composed. The first two types rely on a cantus firmus or 'fixed song' (which may be a sacred or secular tune) around which the composer weaves new material. In the basic Cantus Firmus Mass, the cantus firmus is not altered melodically, though it may be altered rhythmically – for example, spun out in long notes. The second type is the Paraphrase Mass in which the cantus firmus is broken up and orna-mented. In the Alternation Mass plainsong alternates with polyphony. In the Parody Mass an existing piece is re-worked to accommodate the text of each Mass movement. Finally, there is the Freely Composed Mass in which the com-poser invents all his own material. To us today this might seem the most obvious way for a composer to work, yet Medieval and Renaissance composers often preferred to incorporate pre-existing material in their music or to accept the challenge of re-working it.

Palestrina's Mass *Aeterna Christi munera* is a Paraphrase Mass, that is, the cantus firmus is varied rhythmically and melodically throughout the movements. In fact the lines of the hymn-melody or cantus firmus provide the melodic ideas from which the whole Mass is constructed. The cantus firmus itself is the plain-song once associated with the matins hymn *Aeterna Christi munera* – the hymn dating from the twelfth century – and this is how the Mass gets its name. Renaissance Masses were usually named in this way if based on pre-existent material. Thus the Mass *L'homme armé* or *The armed man* – one of the most popular secular tunes used by composers for Mass settings – simply means that the Mass in question is based on that material; Palestrina's Mass *Dies sanctificatus* (Day of holiness) is a Parody Mass for Christmas Day based on a motet of that name by Palestrina himself.

A musical Mass is in five basic movements – although composers may subdivide these. Here is the Latin text (the first movement, *Kyrie eleison* is in fact Greek) with an English translation. Please note that the translation is not always literal; it is a 'compromise' version, familiar to English musicians and composers who, incidentally, normally refer to movements by their Greek or Latin titles. The translation follows closely that in the *Book of Common Prayer* – except where the text itself differs. Our translation does not, therefore, avoid archaic words the most curious of which we further 'translate' in round brackets. The purpose of our translation is to help you to understand Palestrina's music which we must refer to in its Latin setting since in translation the underlay – disposition of words to notes – would vary and be confusing. The *Credo* and two *Agnus Dei* movements are not recorded on the disc but we provide their texts so that you can see the overall plan of the 'musical' Mass.

KYRIE

Kyrie eleison (3), Christe eleison (3),	Lord, have mercy (3), Christ, have mercy (3)
Kyrie eleison (3).	Lord, have mercy (3).

GLORIA

Gloria in excelsis Deo, et	Glory be to God on high, and
in terra pax hominibus bonae voluntatis.	on earth peace to men of good will.
Laudamus Te, benedicimus Te,	We praise Thee, we bless Thee,
adoramus Te, glorificamus Te;	we worship Thee, we glorify Thee;
gratias agimus Tibi	we give thanks to Thee
propter magnam gloriam Tuam,	for Thy great glory,
Domine Deus, Rex coelestis,	Lord God, Heavenly King,
Deus Pater Omnipotens.	God the Father Almighty.
Domine, Fili Unigenite, Jesu Christe,	O Lord, the Only-begotten Son, Jesu Christ
Domine Deus, Agnus Dei,	Lord God, Lamb of God,
Filius Patris,	Son of the Father,

Qui tollis peccata mundi,

miserere nobis;
Qui tollis peccata mundi,

suscipe deprecationem nostram;
Qui sedes ad dexteram Patris,

miserere nobis.
Quoniam Tu solus sanctus,
Tu solus Dominus,
Tu solus altissimus,
Jesu Christe, cum Sancto Spiritu,
in gloria Dei Patris, Amen.

[Thou] that takest away the sins of the world,

Have mercy upon us;
Thou that takest away the sins of the world,

receive our prayer;
Thou that sittest at the right hand of the the Father

have mercy upon us.
For Thou only art holy,
Thou only art the Lord,
Thou only art most high
O Jesus Christ, with the Holy Spirit,
in the glory of God the Father. Amen.

CREDO

Credo in unum Deum,
Patrem omnipotentem, factorem
coeli et terrae,
visibilium omnium et invisibilium;
et in unum Dominum Jesum Christum,
Filium Dei unigenitum,
et ex Patre natum ante omnia saecula.
Deum de Deo, lumen de lumine,
Deum verum de Deo vero,
genitum non factum,
consubstantialem Patri,
per Quem omnia facta sunt.
Qui propter nos homines et
propter nostram salutem descendit de coelis,
et incarnatus est de Spiritu Sancto
ex Maria Virgine, et homo factus est.
Crucifixus etiam pro nobis
sub Pontio Pilato;
passus et sepultus est.
Et resurrexit tertia die,
secundum Scripturas, et ascendit
in coelum;
sedet ad dexteram Patris,
et iterum venturus est cum gloria
judicare vivos et mortuos;

cujus regni non erit finis.
Et in Spiritum Sanctum
Dominum et Vivificantem,
qui ex Patre Filioque procedit;
qui cum Patre et Filio
simul adoratur et conglorificatur;
qui locutus est per Prophetas
Et unam sanctam catholicam et
apolosticam Ecclesiam.
Confiteor unum baptisma
in remissionem peccatorum
et expecto resurrectionem mortuorum
et vitam venturi saeculi. Amen.

I believe in One God
the Father Almighty, maker
of heaven and earth,
and of all things visible and invisible;
and in one Lord Jesus Christ,
the only-begotten Son of God,
begotten of the Father before all worlds,
God of God, light of light,
very (true) God of very (true) God,
begotten not made,
being of one substance with the Father,
by whom all things were made.
Who for us men and
for our salvation came down from heaven,

and was incarnate by the Holy Ghost
of the Virgin Mary, and was made man.
And was crucified also for us
under Pontius Pilate;
He suffered and was buried
And the third day He rose again
according to the Scriptures, and ascended
into Heaven:
and sitteth at the right hand of the Father
and He shall come again with glory to
judge [both] the quick (living) and the dead;

Whose kingdom shall have no end.
And [I believe] in the Holy Ghost,
the Lord and Giver of life
who proceedeth from the Father and Son
who with the Father and [the] Son
together is worshipped and glorified;
who spake by the Prophets.
And in one holy catholic and
apostolic Church.
I acknowledge one baptism
for the remission of sins,
and I look for the resurrection of the dead
and the life of the world to come. Amen.

SANCTUS
(including *Benedictus* and *Hosanna*)

Sanctus, Sanctus,
Sanctus, Dominus Deus Sabaoth:
Pleni sunt coeli et terra gloria Tua.
Hosanna in excelsis. Benedictus
qui venit in nomine Domini.
Hosanna in excelsis.

Holy, Holy,
Holy, Lord God of Hosts:
heaven(s) and earth are full of Thy glory.
Hosanna (praise) in the highest. Blessed
is he that cometh in the name of the Lord
Hosanna in the highest.

AGNUS DEI

Agnus Dei, qui tollis peccata mundi,

miserere nobis . . . Dona nobis pacem.

Lamb of God, who takest away the sins of the world,

have mercy upon us. Grant us Thy peace.

(*Agnus Dei . . . nobis* occurs twice; *Agnus dei . . . mundi* occurs a third time followed by *Dona nobis pacem*. Composers thus often write an *Agnus Dei I* and *Agnus Dei II* to accommodate these variants; or else they may set the whole text in a 'through-composed' manner.)

In his paraphrase Mass *Aeterna Christi munera*, Palestrina uses variations – mostly rhythmic – of the plainsong melody to maintain close thematic links between movements. Here is the plainsong melody *Aeterna Christi munera* on which the Mass is based. **You can hear it sung on side one band 6 of your disc:**

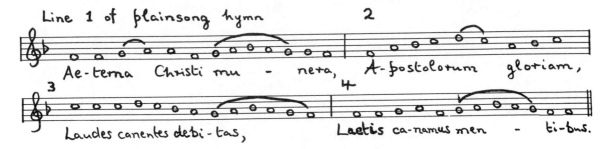

Free translation: Christ's everlasting gifts,
the Apostles' glory,
singing due praises,
let us sing with joyful minds.

We will now consider the Kyrie. **Play band 7 of your disc and follow the first 12 bars of the movement on your score.** As you can both see and hear, the voices enter in an imitative manner, one after the other. If you compare the opening tenor line with the plainsong melody you can see how clearly they are related. The soprano part in bar 7 sounds as if it implies a cadence or resting point in the lower parts, but in fact the entry of the bass part prevents this – deliberately, in order to maintain the flow. In bar 8 the soprano then leads with the plainsong melody and this is imitated by alto (bar 8 last note) and tenor (bar 9 last note). **Listen to band 7 again** and notice how skilfully the entries and cadences are dovetailed.

The *Christe eleison* section is based on the second line of the plainsong and is in a similar, imitative style to the *Kyrie*. Here is the second line of the plainsong hymn, with the opening of the soprano part of the *Christe* beneath it. You can see how the soprano part is derived from the plainsong:

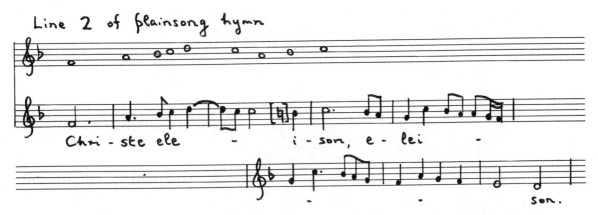

Incidentally, the pleasing shape of Palestrina's melodies, universally admired, is often referred to as the 'Palestrinean curve'; yet the lines of the much older plainsong from which Palestrina derives his material have such curves too. Perhaps the 'Palestrinean curve' merely reflects Palestrina's close affinity with plainsong?

EXERCISE

Band 8 contains the second Kyrie – bars 30–45 of the score. Follow it carefully and note briefly any difference in treatment that Palestrina employs between this Kyrie and the opening one. For example, is it based on the same plainsong and treated imitatively?

SPECIMEN ANSWER

The second Kyrie is also treated imitatively, but this time two motives are introduced almost at once: the first, in the alto, relates to the first line of the plainsong or cantus firmus; one bar later the soprano enters with a motive derived from the third line of the plainsong. This simultaneous use of the two motives continues until the end of the movement.

Let us consider more closely the way in which Palestrina treats his cadences. **Listen to the three cadences on band 9 of your disc:** these are at bars 11–13; 27–29; and 43–45. Here they are in notation with the words omitted:

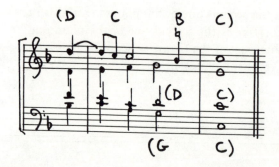

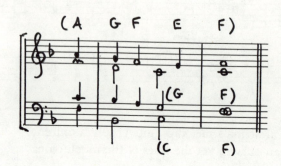

(Remember: the four voice parts reading from top to bottom are Soprano or Treble, Alto, Tenor, Bass.)

EXERCISE

What features do the above cadences have in common? (Pay attention to the penultimate and final chords, and the movement of the soprano part.)

DISCUSSION

We hope you may have noted that each is a 'perfect' cadence with the bass part moving from dominant to tonic in the penultimate and final notes. This is the progression identified in the Introduction to Unit 17. In the second cadence the bass falls five notes (remember, the dominant note is the fifth degree of the scale) to the keynote or tonic; in cadences (a) and (c) to avoid a low F for the bass singer, Palestrina makes the bass rise a fourth, from C to F. This is still the same relationship: dominant-tonic means 'down a fifth' or 'up a fourth'. Next, notice how in each case the soprano or top part moves from the note above the keynote or tonic (the 'supertonic'), through the tonic, to the note below (the 'leading note') and back again to the tonic. Thus in cadences (a) and (c), GFEF; and in cadence (b), DCBC.

Third, the tenor part of each falls supertonic-tonic. All plainsongs end in this way and since in early polyphonic music the tenor part most usually 'held' the plainsong (*tenere* is Latin for 'to hold'), it was bound to end in this way too. Later tenor parts often follow the tradition in plainsong-based music even if the plainsong itself was not confined to the tenor part. Lastly, the rhythmic structure of each cadence is essentially the same. You should be able to hear this and also to see a similarity on paper. A more precise explanation would be that each cadence involves 'preparation', 'suspension', and 'resolution' of the type also identified in the Introduction to Unit 17. By the way, it would not follow that all Palestrinean cadences would be exactly the same, even 'perfect' or ('dominant-tonic') cadences. The bass determines the types, but the parts above may be exchanged or varied. Nevertheless, the above three cadences are entirely representative of Palestrina and of vocal music of this period generally. They are even representative of instrumental music too, though the top part of an instrumental cadence might well be ornamented so that

becomes

There were many permutations of this basic formula.

Having discussed three typical Palestrinean cadences in some detail and now that you have heard them perhaps several times, we want you to test your awareness of this style.

EXERCISE

Play band 10 of your disc and listen to six assorted cadences. They range from the fourteenth to the nineteenth centuries and are all sung unaccompanied, although in fact several are scored by their composers for instruments also. Two of these cadences are by Palestrina. Can you pick out which these are? Listen to all the cadences at least twice.

ANSWER

The third and the fifth.

The six vocal cadences you heard were:

1   From the *Petite Messe Solennelle* (Little Solemn Mass) of 1863 by Rossini (1792–1868).
2   From the *Messe de Nostre Dame* (Mass of Our Lady) of *c.* 1365 by Guillaume de Machaut (1304?–77).
3   From the Mass: *Panis quem ego dabo* (The bread which I shall give you) of 1590 by Palestrina.
4   From the *Missa Solemnis* (Solemn Mass) of 1818–23 by Beethoven (1770–1827).
5   From the Mass *Iste Confessor* (That Champion of the Faith) of 1590 by Palestrina.
6   From the Mass in B minor (1733–38) by J. S. Bach (1685–1750).

So the Palestrina cadences were the third and the fifth.

DISCUSSION

Remember that you were asked to identify two cadences by Palestrina and that you were not required to identify the others. If you reached the correct answer because you felt the other cadences could not have been by Palestrina, then clearly you have grasped the essence of the matter. It was a twofold exercise: first, you should have felt that the third and fifth cadences were likely to be by Palestrina, and then, perhaps on second hearing, the opinion should have been reinforced by your feeling that the other cadences were not by him.

A few words about the other music. Rossini's *Petite Messe Solennelle* is actually a large-scale work scored for choir, soloists, and the refreshingly unusual accompaniment of two pianos and harmonium. The accompaniment was missing in the Kyrie extract but the lovely vocal lines could not have been Palestrina's, largely because of a touch of chromatic harmony of a kind associated with, but by no means confined to, nineteenth-century operatic music. Here is the music:

The chromatic touch occurs half way through bar 2 of the above example.

The second passage was from the Agnus Dei I of one of the earliest known musical settings of the Ordinary of the Mass, composed some two-and-a-quarter centuries before Palestrina's *Aeterna Christi munera*. Perhaps it is the first Medieval music you have heard. If so it may sound strange; yet it is glorious music and would have been made more exciting in performance by the addition of a rich variety of Medieval wind instruments. The cadence is not 'perfect'; indeed it shows none of the characteristics of 'modern' harmony, with its dependence on dominant-tonic relationships which, as we have already observed, first appeared in the Renaissance. Here is the end of the Machaut extract:

The third cadence showed the characteristics already noted in Palestrina's cadences: it is a 'perfect' cadence, the bass descending from dominant to tonic, the tenor falling supertonic to tonic, and the soprano falling from supertonic to tonic, through to the leading note (here ornamented slightly) and back to the tonic. The 'Palestrinean curve' is in evidence, and the deceptively simple-sounding vocal lines together add up to a polyphonic web of great subtlety and beauty.

The next cadence was by Beethoven, and like the previous examples by Rossini and Machaut lacked its instrumental accompaniment. Nevertheless the harmonic basis – as in the Rossini and Machaut again – was complete without it. Beethoven's harmony here is unexceptional, yet too rich for Palestrina. It is in fact in F sharp major, a key Palestrina would never have ventured into (not that you could be expected to know this or indeed to tell what key the extract was in just by hearing it) and the somewhat 'Romantic' qualities of the soprano line, falling to the third at the end, and of the second-inversion chord in the penultimate bar – neither of which would be technically outside Palestrina's limits of style, but which in Beethoven's context are *emotionally* beyond them – rule out the chances of this music being by Palestrina.

The same remarks apply to the fifth cadence as applied to the third and to our previous discussion of Palestrina's style. Here is the music:

The final extract by Bach is from the moving and in some respects exceptional *Crucifixus* movement of his only Mass, a vast work whose composition occupied him about six years. Bach divided the text into twenty-four musical movements. The *Crucifixus* is exceptional in that it is, for Bach's music, unusually chromatic. A four-bar pulsating figure in the orchestral bass underlines the sorrowful text,

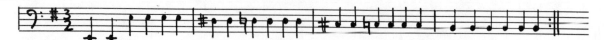

and its falling character, reinforced by poignant appoggiaturas or leaning-notes in the voice-parts, accommodates the words 'crucifixus', 'passus', and 'et sepultus est'. The movement is fifty-four bars long. Our extract (voices only) begins in bar 49 at the final statement of the four-bar bass figure, which in the penultimate bar turns magically from the key of E minor into its brighter relative, G major, in preparation for the joyful movement *Et resurrexit* ('and rose again') which follows. This extract, with its word-painting, its chromatic harmonies, (especially that on the first syllable of the final 'sepultus') and its rich – though restrained – emotional qualities, could not possibly have been composed by Palestrina. Here is the music of the voice-parts (the orchestra doubles them, subdividing each bass note):

You might like to listen to band 10 again in the light of this discussion and re-inforce your feeling for Palestrina's style. The syntax of that style, remember, was by no means unique to Palestrina but was freely used by the more conservative composers of sacred music in the late sixteenth century.

At this point, let us return to Palestrina and hear some more of his music. **Turn to band 1 of your disc where you have the complete performance of the mass: after the Kyrie you can hear the complete Gloria.** (Note that Palestrina – in common with many composers of Masses designed for liturgical use – does not set the opening words of the Gloria and Credo, since they would have been sung to plainsong by the officiating priest. Some 'concert Masses' do include settings of these words.)

EXERCISE

(relating to the Gloria).
1 First, does Palestrina use strands of the plainsong melody? If so, where? If not, why not?
2 Next, can you identify the means by which he varies the texture near the beginning of the movement?
3 Are there any clear instances of word-painting?
4 Finally, can you identify an ornamental cadence similar to that which we mentioned earlier as being often typical of instrumental music of this period?

Use disc and score, perhaps listening first and then reading the score at leisure. Try always to identify what you see with what you hear, no matter how imperfectly. You will improve with practice.

SPECIMEN ANSWER

1 Yes, the plainsong first line appears in the opening bars of the soprano and alto parts.
2 There are several short 'answering' passages in which two voices or parts appear to reply to one another, for example 'Laudamus te', 'Benedicimus te' and 'Adoramus te', 'Glorificamus te', 'Gratias agimus' in bars 6–12. These answering phrases let the air in and achieve lightness, yet they overlap, so the sense of movement is preserved.
3 No, not directly, as far as we can see and hear. Admittedly some repetition of the opening notes of the phrases 'Benedicimus te', 'Adoramus te', 'Glorificamus te', 'Gratias agimus' produce a certain joyful emphasis; it could be argued that in bars 43–45 the tenor and bass are rising appropriately to the words 'Qui sedes ad dexteram Patris' and that the answering, falling soprano phrase 'miserere nobis' brings us back to earth and humanity once more; there is a slight rising in the soprano at 'Altissimus' in bars 53–54; yet one could just as easily demonstrate the opposite at bars 18–19 where the bass part falls to the words 'Rex coelestis' (though admittedly the alto rises). By and large, we do not think there is much evidence of word-painting.
4 Yes, indeed, the soprano 'Amen' (a typical Palestrinean curve) ends with such an ornamented cadence.

DISCUSSION

There is little to add to the above Specimen Answer except to observe that word-painting is somewhat difficult in unaccompanied sacred polyphony where each part is of equal importance. This is because a musical structure, like a building, creates and resolves tensions. If all the parts go in the same direction – downwards for 'descendit de coelis', upwards for 'ascendit in coelum' for example – then the music would probably feel weak. (Composers sometimes make all the parts move in the same direction for reasons appropriate to a particular context, however.) The composer Brahms (1833–97) is said to have placed his hand over the inner parts of a pupil's composition when looking at it for the first time and to have judged it by virtue of its outward parts. If they were strong – and this would be judged partly by the amount of *contrary* movement involved – then the inner ones were probably satisfactory too.

The Sanctus takes the plainsong and makes a further 'paraphrase' or rhythmic variant of each line of it in turn. Here is the opening of the soprano part

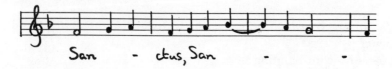

which is imitated at a half-bar's distance by the alto, and later by tenor and bass. At the words 'Domine Deus' Palestrina uses the second line of the hymn; at 'pleni sunt coeli' he derives his melody from the third line. The Benedictus which follows uses only three voices; soprano, alto and tenor. The Hosanna again uses a very similar paraphrase of the plainsong, but the lower voices enter first. This is a short but beautiful movement (or semi-movement), with a particularly pleasing final cadence – not a perfect one, incidentally, but a 'plagal' cadence in which the bass moves from the fourth degree of the scale, the subdominant, to the tonic. **The Sanctus (with Benedictus and Hosanna) can be heard on band 1 following the Gloria.**

There are two *Agnus Dei* movements the second of which accommodates the longer text with the ending 'dona nobis pacem' and is for five voices. Both movements are closely related to the plainsong hymn. The first is peaceful; the second, with its richer texture, is a little more intense and provides a fitting and supremely beautiful conclusion to the whole Mass. We have not recorded these Agnus Dei movements on the disc.

Will you now play the plainsong on band 6 and then the whole of band 1, that is the Kyrie, Gloria and Sanctus movements of Palestrina's Mass Aeterna Christi Munera? Listen critically – that doesn't mean don't enjoy it – and try to hear the relationship of each movement of the Paraphrase Mass with the plainsong on which it is based. Listen also to how admirably the vocal lines weave their polyphonic web; listen also to the word-setting which, although by no means exclusively syllabic, is nevertheless sensitive and restrained. Do you think Hawkins, Schumann, Gounod and others were guilty of exaggeration in what they wrote about Palestrina?

2   Motet: Ave verum corpus (Hail true body) by William Byrd (1543–1623)

William Byrd was born at Lincoln and at the early age of twenty became organist of the cathedral there, a post he held for about ten years. In 1570 he was appointed a Gentleman of the Chapel Royal in London and later became co-organist with Thomas Tallis (*c.* 1505–1585). For a couple of years Byrd

Figure 13 William Byrd. From a rare engraving of c. 1729 in the British Museum after V. Haym, by G. Vandergucht (Radio Times Hulton Picture Library).

retained his Lincoln appointment also – it was not unusual to hold more than one appointment at the same time – but he gave it up late in 1572.

EXERCISE

Since it was not unusual for composers and others to hold more than one appointment simultaneously, why should Byrd have given up the important post of organist of Lincoln cathedral after his appointment to the Chapel Royal?

DISCUSSION

No need for a Specimen Answer, because you have surely given the most likely reason for Byrd's resignation from Lincoln: London and Lincoln are a hundred and thirty miles apart, and notwithstanding what we have said in Unit 17 about the mobility of Renaissance artists, it would hardly have been practicable for Byrd to commute on horseback between these two cities, even if he had spent a substantial amount of time at each. In fact, the flat, orderly, agricultural fen country of Cambridgeshire, the Isle of Ely, and Lincolnshire that we can see today would have presented a very different aspect before the land was drained successfully in the seventeenth century. (There is one surviving area preserved in its original state, a National Trust nature reserve at Wicken, Cambridgeshire.) The Icknield Way, running from Salisbury to the Wash and dating from 6,000 or 5,000 B.C., long remained the sole line of communication from Southern England and it would presumably have been along this windswept, damp and chilly route that Byrd would have had to travel. Also it is possible that, in the court circle, he felt more secure from vexation for his recusancy.

Five years after Byrd's appointment to the Chapel Royal, Queen Elizabeth granted him and Tallis a monopoly of printing and selling music, a monopoly Byrd retained after Tallis' death. Byrd and Tallis were close associates and friends notwithstanding their forty-year difference in ages and Tallis was godfather to Byrd's second son who was called Thomas after him. Furthermore, Byrd seems to have been a pupil of Tallis – certainly we may regard him as a pupil by influence even if he was not one in actual fact. Byrd and Tallis thus worked together as organists of the Chapel Royal, at their Printing Monopoly, and in the composition and production of a set of motets entitled *Cantiones Sacrae* (Sacred Songs) of 1551 – altogether a remarkable and fruitful association.

In the early 1570s Byrd had acquired property in Essex at Stapleford Abbotts, not far from Epping, and ten miles south-east of Waltham Abbey where Tallis had been organist until its dissolution; soon after, Byrd was involved in one of his several lawsuits. Another arose in connection with the lease of the Manor of Langley, Gloucestershire, which Queen Elizabeth granted him in 1579, 'out of her princely bounty . . . to gratify the service of the said William Byrd.' It was probably the money accruing from the Langley property which enabled Byrd to take up residence at Harlington, then a peaceful village a few miles west of London and reasonably convenient for Byrd's duties at Greenwich or Whitehall; now Harlington is adjacent to London's Heathrow airport.

In 1591 Byrd had been occupied with a third lawsuit, this time concerning property in Berkshire. Byrd's lawsuits – six in all – are complicated, but although he seems to have had right on his side their results were seldom satisfactory for him. In 1593 Byrd moved back to Essex, to Stondon Massey, five miles or so from his other property at Stapleford Abbotts. At first he leased the Stondon property but after a long dispute in which again Byrd seems to have been unjustly treated, he bought the property outright in 1610. Byrd lived at Stondon Massey until his death and during his last years appears to have lived in semi-retirement, although he remained on the payroll of the Chapel Royal. Furthermore, at the time of his death he had also apartments in Lord Worcester's house in the Strand. This and much other detailed information can be found in *William Byrd* by E. H. Fellowes.

Byrd died on 4 July 1623. His life had been exceptionally busy both musically and domestically. He had married twice (his first wife appears to have died shortly after 1586) and had five children. He spent time and energy on six lawsuits. He had composed a particularly large amount of music: three Masses; nearly two hundred and fifty motets of which about one hundred and ninety were published during his lifetime in the three volumes of *Cantiones Sacrae* and two of *Gradualia*; sixty-five anthems, and other Anglican church music including four services; about a hundred and fifty sacred and secular songs, a hundred of which appeared in *Psalms, Sonets and songs* of 1588, *Songs of sundrie natures* of 1589 and *Psalmes, Songs and Sonnets* of 1611; canons and rounds; thirty or forty pieces of string ensemble music, and over a hundred pieces of keyboard music. He had been active also as performer and teacher.

Clearly, Byrd was a more all-round composer than Palestrina, yet he was hardly less successful in every field that he attempted. His Masses are comparable to the best composed on the continent; his motets, of all kinds, large and small, simple and complex, reach the highest limits of musical expression; his other vocal music contains many outstanding works, characterized by a tunefulness which seems a curiously English trait – notwithstanding the polyphonic structure, the treble part nevertheless frequently has a genuine tune. (A perfect example of this English characteristic is found in Orlando Gibbons' *The silver swan* which we shall examine later in this unit.) Byrd's string music is no less remarkable than his keyboard music for invention and skill of construction.

Palestrina's admirers stress the 'spiritual' qualities of his music – it seems almost to have been fashioned in heaven. Yet the less detached, more human nature of Byrd's art is perhaps what enables us to perceive its qualities the more easily. Indeed, when performing Byrd's music it is possible to feel close to its composer; we find it hard to imagine quite the same affinity with Palestrina, notwithstanding wholehearted admiration and respect.

A single commendation will serve for William Byrd, that of his pupil and friend Thomas Morley, composer and author of *A Plain and Easy Introduction to Practical Music*, already mentioned in Unit 17. Morley said of Byrd that he was 'never without reverence to be named among the musicians' – a sentiment that seems to have been generally observed.

As you know already, Byrd's motet *Ave verum corpus* was published in 1605. Here is the Latin poem with a fairly literal translation:

Ave verum corpus,	Hail true body,
natum de Maria Virgine;	born of the Virgin Mary;
vere passum immolatum in	[which] truly suffered, being offered upon
cruce pro homine;	the cross for man's sake;
cuius latus perforatum	whose pierced side
unda fluxit et sanguine;	flowed with water and with blood;
esto nobis praegustatum	be a strengthening food
in mortis examine.	for us in the trial of death.
O dulcis, O pie,	O dear one, O loving one,
O Jesu Fili Mariae;	O Jesus Son of Mary,
miserere mei. Amen.	have mercy on me. Amen.

EXERCISE

Play band 11 of your disc and listen to Byrd's setting of the first line of the poem. Follow the score too. (The barring has been added by the editor to make the score easier to read. The original was not barred.) Write down what you notice about:

(a)   word-setting (this means correspondence of music to text, *not* word-painting)

(b)   the soprano or treble part

(c)   the cadence in the last two bars.

SPECIMEN ANSWER

(a)   Without any obvious devices to attract attention to a particular word – for example, 'Ave' ('Hail') could have been set loudly, or else repeated to achieve emphasis – Byrd's music seems to fit the text perfectly. There is a slight emphasis on the first syllable of 'verum' ('true') which seems particularly appropriate. A highly devotional mood is established immediately with utmost economy of means.

(b)   The soprano or treble part has a narrow range of four notes (highest A, lowest E) which creates smoothness appropriate to a prayer of this kind. The melody of the last two bars is ornamented in an almost 'instrumental' manner.

(c)   The cadence is 'perfect' with the bass rising from dominant to tonic.

The tenor is suspended over the bar line on the first syllable of 'verum' and then, after falling, rises very beautifully to B♮ – the major third. This makes a subtle contrast with the preceding B♭s.

DISCUSSION

(a) Byrd's setting of texts – what musicians refer to as 'word-setting' – is of the highest order. Like a painter who can create the right mood with a single stroke of a brush, Byrd can induce the right atmosphere with the simplest musical means. It seems this was a gift, for in the Dedication of the 1605 book of *Gradualia* to Lord Northampton he commented that if the pieces that followed were successful it was not because of his own skill, but because of the inspiration of the words themselves. In *William Byrd* Fellowes, in his own translation, quotes from that Latin dedication as follows:

> for there is a certain hidden power, as I learnt from experience, in the thoughts underlying the words themselves; so that, as one meditates upon the sacred words and constantly and seriously considers them, the right notes, in some inexplicable manner, suggest themselves quite spontaneously.

Byrd obtained the slight emphasis on the first syllable of 'verum' by following a D major chord with a F major one – that is, by the juxtaposition of the F♯ (soprano, first note of bar 2) and the F♮ (bass, last note of bar 2). This is a particularly English characteristic and is sometimes known as a 'false relation'. There are further examples in this motet. We do not think it necessary to comment on (b) or (c).

EXERCISE

Band 12 contains bars 31 (last beat) to 38.

In the setting of the words 'O dulcis, O pie, O Jesu Fili Mariae' will you please
(a)   identify further 'false relations' and say why you think Byrd introduces them;
(b)   comment on the texture of bars 35–38 ('O pie! O Jesu fili Mariae');
(c)   comment on the soprano part, bars 34–41 ('O Jesu fili Mariae, miserere mei . . .').

SPECIMEN ANSWER

(a)   There are 'false relations' though not very acute ones – in bars 33 (tenor B♮ followed by soprano B♭) and 34–35 (alto B♮, bar 34, followed by bass B♭, first note of 35). Byrd probably wrote them to create a feeling of anguish or fervour of this crucial point of the prayer.
(b)   The texture of bars 32–35 is simple enough, though highly effective: the soprano leads each time (the boys' voices for whom the music was intended in liturgical use signifying innocence) and the lower three parts respond.
(c)   The soprano part echoes the poem exactly: two short phrases ('O dulcis, O pie') are followed by a longer one ('O Jesu Fili Mariae'). Byrd further heightens the spirit of the third by stretching out the words a little and thus extending the musical phrase.

DISCUSSION

There is little to add except to draw your attention to the subtle rhythms of this music. Byrd's polyphonic style represents an ideal marriage of linear and vertical components: each vocal line has individuality and room to develop, yet merges beautifully with its partner.

EXERCISE

Band 13 contains bars 39–46, the music of 'miserere mei'. Play this band and discuss Byrd's setting of these words. This time you should make your response entirely in your own terms, though you may find it helpful to refer to previous exercises for guidelines.

SPECIMEN ANSWER

The musical setting of 'miserere mei' seems destined for these words. The four-note motive for 'miserere', shaped like an arch, seems to correspond exactly to the accentuation of the word itself, yet heighten its intensity. There are 'false relations' – quite acute ones – in bars 40 and 44; in fact the F♮ in bar 40 is heard before the F♯ ceases sounding, so there is an actual F♯/F♮ clash. This again heightens the tensions and emotion of the prayer 'miserere mei'. The texture is interesting at bar 40 onwards: the alto and tenor lead, and a bar later the bass replies, yet the soprano enters half-a-bar later, overlapping with the bass. The alto repeats the prayer at bar 41, overlapping with the soprano's phrase; the tenor and bass follow similarly. There is a 'perfect' cadence at bars 45–46, not unlike that found at bars 3–4, but extended and a little more involved.

DISCUSSION

If you noted (a) sensitive word-setting (b) 'false relations', (c) imitative or overlapping phrases (d) varied textures (resulting from the answering phrases) then you certainly have identified the most important points. Yet remember that we only look closely at music to help us understand and appreciate it more in performance – so don't let this kind of analysis become too fascinating!

Now play the whole motet Ave Verum on band 2.

You will notice that the passage we have just been discussing is repeated and that there is a slight adjustment near the end to make the final cadence long and tender. Under a held soprano part the others at last find a resting-place.

3   Madrigal: Baci soavi e cari (Kisses, tender and dear) by Claudio Monteverdi (1567–1643)

We come now to the first of three secular voice pieces each of which we shall treat more briefly than the sacred ones, relying on the pieces themselves to demonstrate the close correspondence of text and music which composers of madrigals and part-songs sought and frequently achieved.

The madrigal was born in Italy, a noble offspring of the popular frottola. The frottola was a strophic song, generally composed for three or four voices and marked by clear-cut rhythms and simple harmony. Many appeared also for

solo voice and lute accompaniment. Frottola texts were not usually distinguished and it was the revival of literary taste, fostered by the Venetian nobleman and scholar Cardinal Bembo (1470–1547) which was largely responsible
for the emergence of the madrigal. Bembo aimed to restore the Italian language to its former glory in the time of Dante (1265–1321), Petrarch (1304–
74) – who is discussed in Units 5–6, Section 3.1 – and Boccaccio (1313–75).
Petrarch in particular was the model for Bembo's own poetry and he soon
became the most popular poet of the new madrigal composers. Among other
poets they admired and set were Ariosto, whose celebrated *Orlando Furioso*
was published in 1516, Trissimo, Cassola, Guarini, Tasso, and Bembo himself.

Clearly then, the Italian madrigal was at first a literary creation. Poets and
musicians alike realized how both words and music could interact to create
a new art form worthy of their own ideals and suited to the sophisticated tastes
of Italian Renaissance aristocracy. The madrigal differed from the frottola
not only in the elevated character of its verse, but musically as well, for whereas
the frottola had been simple and tuneful with the soprano part prominent,
the madrigal was more genuinely polyphonic. Indeed its sectional, overlapping,
method of treating the text was not far removed from the style of Mass and
motet. This aspect owed much to the fact that there were many Netherlands
composers skilled in polyphonic writing working in Italy at this time. Yet
polyphony was not slavishly observed as was sometimes the case in sacred
music, but was used freely in conjunction with homophonic or chordal writing
where appropriate to the spirit of the text. In each case, the aim was for each
voice to declare the text in as beautiful a manner as possible. The composer
and theorist Zarlino (a pupil of Willaert and who likewise became director
of music at St. Mark's Venice) in his *Istituzioni armoniche* (Principles of harmony)
of 1555 gave instructions for word-setting which are quoted in translation in
Denis Arnold's *Marenzio* as follows:

> . . . cheerful harmonies and swift rhythms must be used for cheerful matters, and for
> sad matters, sad harmonies and slow rhythms, so that all may be done fittingly. The
> musician, therefore, should be warned to accompany, so far as he can, every word in
> such a manner that when it denotes severity, harshness, cruelty, bitterness and other
> such things, the harmony should be like this also – that is, to some extent harsh and hard,
> yet not so greatly as to offend. Similarly, when any word expresses complaint, grief,
> affliction, sighs, tears and so on, let the harmony be full of sadness . . .

The earliest madrigals were not far removed from the frottola, as the opening
bars of *Quandro ritrova* (known in an English version as *Down in a flowery vale*)
by the Roman composer Constanzo Festa (*c.* 1490–1545) demonstrate. The
music is chordal and strongly rhythmic:

Other leading early madrigal composers included the Netherlanders Verdelot
(*c.* 1480–*c.* 1540), Willaert, who we have mentioned previously as director of
music at St. Mark's Venice, and Arcadelt (*c.* 1505–*c.* 1560).

Yet by Arcadelt's time, and in his own madrigals, word-painting, polyphony,
and a growing intensity of expression were apparent. The next generation, led

by Willaert's successor at St. Mark's, Cipriano de Rore (1516–1565) developed the madrigal into its mature form. De Rore published eight books of madrigals, three for four voices, and five for the increasingly popular combination of five voices. Typically, his favourite poet was Petrarch. Highly descriptive word-painting, chromaticism, dramatic harmonic effects and sudden changes of speed became more prominent and reached their artistic limits in the virtuosic madrigal composers, Marenzio, Gesualdo, and Monteverdi. Gesualdo, incidentally, was exceptional in his lack of literary taste in his madrigal settings – he seemed to regard the text merely as necessary raw material for his music. He was equally exceptional in his experimental and sometimes eccentric music.

As we have noted earlier, the first collection of Italian madrigals published in England was Nicholas Yonge's *Musica Transalpina* of 1588. The texts were given in translation. Several further collections of Italian madrigals appeared in the next few years. A madrigalian form took root in England and during a period of about twenty-five years, flowered in a most astonishing way. The term 'madrigal' was used loosely in England by both poets and composers – not surprisingly, considering its confused etymological origins well summarized by Fellows in chapter five of *The English Madrigal Composers*. This etymological problem prevents a just and direct comparison between the Italian and English types. As Joseph Kerman observes in his penetrating study *The Elizabethan Madrigal*, only two English composers, John Wilbye (1574–1638) and John Ward (?–c. 1640) showed a literary taste of the kind common to their Italian colleagues. By and large, English composers ignored the 'new poets' such as Spenser, Sidney, Drayton and Shakespeare, and chose instead light verse in the Italian style – or else, like Thomas Campian the lute-song composer, wrote their own poetry. The term 'English song' – which, according to Kerman is 'an abstract composition that obeys purely musical rather than literary dictates' – would perhaps be more appropriate for the 'madrigalian' compositions of many of the English composers, including Byrd and Gibbons.

Certainly, as Professor Kerman rightly points out, the literary element was never regarded so highly in England as in Italy. Yet to use this as an argument for comparing the English composers unfavourably with their Italian counterparts seems to us somewhat misleading. The Italian composers were catering for the numerous aristocratic establishments of the Italian principalities. In England, as you know, there was only one court: there was also an increasingly important middle-class. English 'madrigalian' publications catered for both. It is therefore hardly surprising that their music was less esoteric than the Italian, more conservative, more restrained, more homely, and in general, more tuneful. Yet paradoxically, the typically English understatement found in a piece like Orlando Gibbons' *The silver swan* may yield – to English ears at least – a particularly intense response. Let us now turn to the three madrigalian pieces we have chosen for examination.

Claudio Monteverdi (1567–1643)

Monteverdi is one of the outstanding composers in the history of Western music and certainly the leading figure of the transitional period from Renaissance to Baroque. He is perhaps best known today as the first major opera composer: two operas, *Orfeo* (Orpheus) first performed in Mantua in 1607, and *L'incoronazione di Poppea* (The Coronation of Poppea), first performed in Venice in 1642, are probably the earliest which are currently in the operatic repertoire today. But these belong stylistically and chronologically to the

Figure 14 Claudio Monteverdi, by Bernardo Strozzi (Tiroler Landesmuseum Ferdinandeum, Innsbruck).

Baroque era – as do the last five books of madrigals – whereas we are concerned with music he composed in late Renaissance style. You will appreciate that the claims we made for both Palestrina and Byrd do not conflict with those made for Monteverdi, for not only was Monteverdi born considerably later, but the chronological gap between them is further emphasized by the fact that neither Byrd nor Palestrina was a particularly progressive composer whereas Monteverdi was undoubtedly so – in fact, he has been called the 'father of modern music'.

Monteverdi's life was outwardly uneventful. Born in Cremona, about fifty miles south-east of Milan, he first studied with the director of music at his local cathedral. In 1590 he entered the service of Vincenzo Gonzaga, Duke of Mantua, and in 1599 accompanied him to Flanders, meeting a number of French musicians there. In 1602 Monteverdi became director of music of the ducal chapel. From 1613 until his death he was director of music at St. Mark's, Venice, having joined the priesthood in 1631.

Monteverdi's earlier madrigals followed the examples set by Marenzio, but certain techniques he employed give a glimpse of the operatic style which was to follow. We find favourite devices that are not necessarily typical of madrigals alone which reveal his strong dramatic sense. His free use of dissonance (discord) surprised and even shocked his contemporaries. Other dramatic devices included exclamatory themes and chordal chantings of a particular phrase.

Baci soavi e cari comes from his first book of madrigals, published in Venice in 1587 when he was only twenty. Here is the Italian poem by Giambattista Guarini (1538–1612) with an English translation kindly made for us by Dr. Giovanni Carsaniga, Reader in Italian Studies at The University of Sussex. As with *Aeterna Christi munera*, we shall refer to the music in its Italian setting because of the close relationship of words and music.

Baci, soavi e cari,	Kisses, tender and dear,
Cibi della mia vita,	food of my life,
C'hor m'involate, hor mi rendete il core,	that now steal, now give me back my heart,
Per voi convien ch'impari	I have come to learn through you
Come un'alma rapita	that an enraptured soul
Non senta il duol di morte, e pur si more.	does not feel the pangs of death, even while it's dying.
Quant 'ha di dolce amore!	How much sweetness is there in Love!
Perché sempr'io vi baci,	This is why I always kiss you,
O dolcissime rose!	O [lips as] sweet [as] roses.
In voi tutto riposo,	All [sweetness] resides in you
Et s'io potessi ai vostri dolci baci	And if I could, through your sweet kisses,
La mia vita finire,	end my life,
O che dolce morire.	what a sweet death it would be!

Band 3 of your disc contains the complete madrigal.

We think that what will have impressed you – even if you were not fully aware of everything that was going on – is the firmly wedded partnership of words and music. The varying speeds and accents of the music are directly governed by the meaning and accentuation of the words. Monteverdi was already carrying out principles he later defended from the attacks of the reactionary critic Artusi in the preface to his (Monteverdi's) *Fifth Book of Madrigals* of 1605 in which he stated that 'the modern composer builds on the foundations of truth' and Monteverdi mentions there that he has prepared a reply entitled *Seconda Prattica, ovvero, Perfezioni della Moderna Musica* (Second Practice, or Perfection of Modern Music). It seems that this reply was never written, although Monteverdi's brother, Giulio Cesare, wrote at length about the 'Second Practice' in his *Dichiarazione* (Declaration), itself a reply to a further attack by Artusi based on Monteverdi's preface to the 1605 publication. This reply is given in *Source Readings in Music History*.[1] Giulio Cesare writes that his brother considered that the harmony, instead of 'being the mistress [as in older music of the First Practice] becomes the servant of the words, and the words the mistress of the harmony, to which way of thinking the Second Practice, or modern usage, tends'.

Let us return to *Baci soavi e cari* and look more closely at several sections. **Play band 14 of your disc and listen to bars 1–26 particularly carefully following the score also.** You will surely agree that the inflection of the words is mirrored in the rhythm of the music.

[1] Quoted in translation in O. Strunk, *Source Readings in Music History* W. W. Norton and Co. New York 1950; available in five paperback volumes (the Monteverdi extracts appear in the third), 1965.

And when there is a word of more importance than those preceding it, the vocal line moves to point it, as in 'soavi, e *cari*' and 'cibi della mia *vita*'. And again when we reach a more thoughtful and serious line the note values themselves slow down to make both an aural and visual change, as in 'non senta il duoldi morte pur si more' (bars 14–26). In fact, from bar 26 onwards for many bars the rhythmic flow and pointing of the words is such as to transcend bar lines (which the editor has added for ease in reading).

EXERCISE

Listen to the complete madrigal on band 3.

Fairly obviously, this music differs from the Palestrina Mass and the Byrd motet we examined earlier. Remember, *Aeterna Christi munera* was published three years after the madrigal, and *Ave verum corpus* eighteen years after it. Yet, avoiding the obvious point of secular versus sacred, can you identify any other broad differences between the Monteverdi madrigal and the pieces by Palestrina and Byrd? You might find it helpful to make your notes under the headings

(a)   does this early Monteverdi madrigal seem older or newer in style than the other, later pieces? What reasons can you give?

(b)   Can you find anything that seems unsatisfactory and would support the argument that Monteverdi was too young and inexperienced at this time to be considered seriously as a prominent and typical later madrigal composer?

SPECIMEN ANSWER

(a)   The music seems to ebb and flow more obviously than that by Palestrina or Byrd which we examined and this is largely because the word-painting is more deliberate. (Examples of this have already been identified.) No doubt this is partly explained by the fact that the madrigal is a secular piece and the other two were sacred – yet this is not a complete answer. Monteverdi's close reflection of the words in this music is a 'progressive' characteristic which was to lead him eventually to the highly dramatic style of his seventeenth-century 'Baroque' music. Thus *Baci soavi e cari* seems a 'newer' more 'modern' piece than *Aeterna Christi munera* or *Ave verum corpus* despite its earlier date of publication.

(b)   There are seemingly unrelated chords juxtaposed from time to time (for example, end of bar 3, beginning of bar 4; bar 12, first and second chords; bar 32, second chord and bar 33) and some sudden ornamental flourishes that seem almost fussy (bar 9, alto; 37, tenor; 48 and 64, second soprano and alto) and there are also many high notes for the first soprano, including a top A in bar 36: yet all these elements contribute to, rather than detract from, the overall impression that the composer knows precisely what he wanted and had the technique to accomplish it. No, we do not think Monteverdi could be faulted here on grounds of youth or inexperience: quite the opposite in fact – *Baci soavi e cari* is an authoritative piece by an accomplished composer.

DISCUSSION

There is little to add. As we have observed, there are 'progressive' tendencies in Monteverdi's early music which were later to lead to his 'Second Practice'.

It is easy to be wise after the event and the Specimen Answer may be said to suffer from the gift of hindsight. Given this madrigal alone and no supporting evidence, could we make such claims for it? Perhaps not, but in any case we would not want to make excessive claims for any Mass, motet or madrigal of this period. There are so many first-rate pieces it would be unwise to focus attention too closely on any single one and maintain that it alone represented a tradition or pointed the way to the future.

Will you now bear in mind all we have observed so far, and play the complete madrigal again? Please follow the score at the same time.

4   Madrigal: April is in my mistress' face by Thomas Morley (1558–1603)

We have already met Thomas Morley, the devoted pupil and friend of William Byrd, composer, and the author of *A Plain and Easy Introduction to Practical Music*. Not much is known of Morley's life, but he was organist of (old) St. Paul's Cathedral in 1591 and a Gentleman of the Chapel Royal in 1592. Morley composed splendid church music (to Latin and English words) yet is probably best remembered today for his canzonets (light madrigals), madrigals, ballets (a type of English frottola and usually having a 'fa la' refrain), 'consort lessons' (music for mixed ensemble), lute-songs, and also as editor of *The Triumphs of Oriana*. This was a collection of twenty-five madrigals published in 1601, supposedly in honour of Queen Elizabeth. The publication was doubtless inspired by the Italian collection *Il trionfo di Dori* of 1592.

As we noted in Unit 17, Morley founded the English madrigal school. His *First Booke of Madrigalls to Foure Voyces* of 1594 was the first English publication to use the word 'madrigal' on its title page, and since *April is in my mistress' face* is the first piece in this collection, it can be considered the first English madrigal. Morley was not only the first English madrigal composer however, he was also the most important and influential. In *The Elizabethan Madrigal* Professor Kerman writes (pp. 130–1):

> Thomas Morley was the first and most important of the English madrigalists, and the closest of all to the music of Italy. The reasons for his fame and subsequent influence were many. A pupil and friend of William Byrd, he was an established London musician, first at St Paul's and later at court, where his friends and patrons seem to have been of some influence; his services were significant enough to gain him the powerful position of monopolist of music printing in 1597, after Byrd's patent expired. He was the first English composer to issue sets of madrigals and canzonets, and, judging from the number of his publications, by far the most prolific composer of these varieties; his work must have been doubly influential because in the first five years of his activity (1593–97) he was the only Englishman publishing madrigals at all. By 1597, when the next composers came to the presses, Morley had already instituted the English madrigal school with five popular sets, to be followed by two Italian anthologies and *The Triumphs of Oriana*. His work was especially well liked in the first decades of the new century, as we know from the many editions of his sets that were demanded – such reprints were particularly rare for English music at this time. Morley's prestige must have been much increased by his impressive theoretical work, *A Plain and Easy Introduction to Practical Music* of 1597, which went to a second edition in 1608. In learning and scope this book stands head and shoulders above any other musical treatise published in Elizabethan England, and it was a standard didactic text for many years.
>
> Morley was exactly of the generation to be most impressed by the influx of Italian culture in the 1570s and 1580s. He was born in 1557 or 1558, within six years of Sidney, Spenser, and Watson; in 1580 he was at the beginning of his career, no doubt as receptive as other Englishmen of the time to the exciting novel poetry and music of the Italian courts.

No other musicians of Morley's generation distinguished themselves in Italianate composition, and the younger men looked instinctively to him as their model. But Morley looked instinctively to Italy; his historic position is that of a pioneer who digested the Continental style, naturalized it, and presented it to his countrymen in a form that they could immediately appreciate and utilize further. It is first of all from this point of view that Morley's work should be approached. Morley set the tone definitively for a class of composition that is characteristic of the English books that came after him. The popularity and cultivation of the English madrigal was in large measure due to him alone.

April is in my mistress' face is a translation of *Nel vis'ha un vago Aprile* by the composer-poet Orazio Vecchi (1550–1605). It is a very short poem and Morley repeats lines of it to extend the music, repeating both the text and music of the last line. Here is the poem:

April is in my mistress' face
And July in her eyes hath place,
Within her bosom is September,
But in her heart a cold December.

'July', by the way, was pronounced to rhyme with 'duly' – like today's name 'Julie'.

Morley's music is as unpretentious as the poem. It begins with a short phrase for the upper two voices, the rhythm of which follows that of the words. The lower voices join in at bar 3, loosely imitating the opening phrase, but following it more closely at their second entry in bar 6. **Play band 15 of the disc and hear and follow Morley's setting of the opening line of the poem.**

Morley's setting of the second line, 'And July in her eyes hath place' also begins with the two upper voices singing in thirds. The lower voices reply, but almost immediately the upper voices interrupt, and a delightful cadence is reached at the second occurrence of the words 'hath place' at bars 14–15. Incidentally, this cadence is in B♭ major, the relative major of the home key, G minor – a thoroughly 'progressive' tonal move. Try to hear how satisfactory this tonal relationship is when you later play the complete piece.

'Within her bosom is September' is not remarkable, textually or musically, although the paired upper voices swinging to the cadence over the long held notes of the lower voices (bars 21–23) might be considered as an example of mildly erotic word-painting. (The poet was clearly making a comparison between the lady's bosom and ripe autumnal fruit.)

EXERCISE

Now play the whole madrigal on band 4 of your disc and, as always, follow the score. What are the principal features of the final bars (23–end), starting at the words 'But in her heart'?

SPECIMEN ANSWER

The principal features of the closing section are the repeated-note motive 'But in her heart' and the way Morley uses it imitatively. For example, the soprano leads with this figure in bar 23, the tenor follows in the same bar, the bass follows in the next bar, and one bar later (25) soprano and alto enter together with the same motive; and so on. There is no very obvious word-painting of the kind one might have expected to be associated with the phrase 'cold December', – bleak, empty harmonies, for example – although possibly the repeated-note idea represents driving rain or hailstones.

DISCUSSION

We described the music earlier as unpretentious, and the final section is in keeping with this. The repeated-note idea, used in loose imitation, is its chief characteristic. Apart from the 'hailstone' suggestion we've made there is no overt evidence of word-painting. A lost opportunity? Possibly, but Morley treats the piece so lightly, it seems probable he deliberately avoided the baser temptations of 'a cold December', thinking that to succumb would be to give the madrigal a seriousness it hardly deserved.

5   Part-song: The silver swan by Orlando Gibbons (1583–1625)

Figure 15 Orlando Gibbons, Music School, Oxford (Radio Times Hulton Picture Library).

This astonishingly beautiful piece, the text of which is anonymous, is the opening number of *The First Set of Madrigals and Motets of 5 Parts* by Orlando Gibbons, published in 1612. In fact, it was Gibbons' only set; furthermore, the pieces in it are strictly neither madrigals nor motets, but rather, serious part-songs. (We shall give an account of Gibbons' life in Unit 19.)

EXERCISE

Play band 16 of the disc and hear the complete piece. Can you describe its overall musical plan?

SPECIMEN ANSWER

The piece falls into three main sections (bars 1–7, 7–14, 14–22). Yet there are really only two musical sections since the second is repeated; so we could regard the musical form as ABB.

We will look at the first section, bars 1–7, more closely. It maintains a fairly equal balance between homophony and polyphony, with the main melodic interest in the soprano part constantly challenged by beautiful independent lines in the lower parts. Take, for example, the two lowest parts:

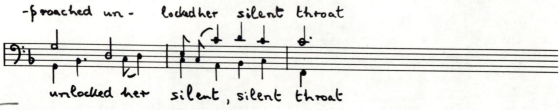

Although not as self-sufficient or interesting melodically as the soprano part there are certainly some pleasing moments: for example, at bars 3 and 4 of the first bass part; and the charming cross-accent in the second bass part at bar 5 ('unlocked her') where phased wording causes some unexpected cross-accents.

Play that band again and see if you can follow the bass parts of the opening section.

Moving on to the second section, 'leaning her breast against the reedy shore', you can notice how the parts enter imitatively, yet closely so that the effect of leaning is built up to a small climax on 'against' with an unusual discord on the first beat of bar 10. The following phrase 'Thus sang her first and last' is treated also in closely dovetailed imitation with some lovely cross-accents and an especially charming sequence of falling fifths in the tune. Look more closely at the cadence at bars 13–14. Notice how, as with the typical Palestrina cadence, although there is movement in the upper and middle parts the fundamental movement in the lowest or second bass part (the part that determines the harmony – that is the choice of notes above) is basically C to F, or dominant to tonic. As you now know, this forms what is called a 'perfect' cadence. Now compare these perfect cadences by Gibbons and Palestrina and see how similar they are.

(a) Gibbons, *The silver swan* bars 13–14.

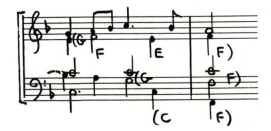

(b) Palestrina, Kyrie from *Aeterna Christi munera* bars 11–13.

(c) Palestrina, *idem*, bars 43–45.

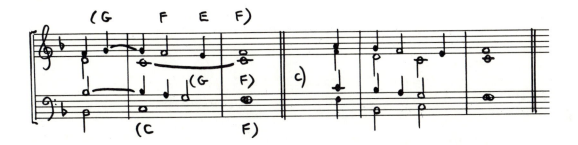

EXERCISE

Now play band 16 of your disc and comment on the material in it.

SPECIMEN ANSWER

The material is the same as the section 'leaning her breast', with an imitative opening on 'Farewell' and this time the discord which previously occurred on '*against*' falls more purposefully on the word 'death'.

DISCUSSION

No doubt Gibbons used this striking discord deliberately to underline the word 'death'. It certainly makes its point. Yet it is strange that he anticipated it at 'a-*gainst* the reedy shore'. If we look at the form of the poem:

	Rhyme
The silver swan, who living had no note,	A
When death approached unlocked her silent throat,	A
Leaning her breast against the reedy shore,	B
Thus sung her first and last, and sung no more,	B
Farewell all joys, O death come close mine eyes,	C
More geese than swans now live, more fools than wise.	C

we can see that it divides itself up clearly into three sections. Gibbons, for musical reasons has chosen to take his form A (first two lines), B (third and fourth lines), B (fifth and sixth lines), which makes him anticipate that striking effect on the word 'death'. However the very satisfying shape of the piece, with its falling cadences more than compensates for this. **Band 5, you remember, contains this madrigal complete.**

This part-song has been unceasingly popular since it was first composed and published some three-and-a-half centuries ago. It seems to have virtually every quality that one could hope for in such a composition: a satisfactory and (we think) moving text; outward musical simplicity which disguises the impeccable craftsmanship of the five-part writing; a natural and beautiful melodic line which nevertheless remains only a part of the polyphonic whole; and finally, a disarming brevity. It is as if Gibbons, in a single flash of inspiration, summed up the creative endeavours of a whole era of musical composition. What do you think?

UNIT 19   RENAISSANCE MUSIC PART III

Introduction

We shall examine four pieces of music: a very short piece of 'programme' music; a pavan and galliard pair; a prelude and fantasia pair; a set of variations. This yields six forms commonly found in Renaissance instrumental music. The composers of all but the variations are English: William Byrd (1543–1623), Giles Farnaby (c. 1565–1625) and Orlando Gibbons (1583–1625). The variations are by a continental composer, Jan Pieterszoon Sweelinck (1562–1621) of Amsterdam. I shall give the reasons for this last choice when discussing the variations.

1   Giles Farnaby's Dream by Giles Farnaby (c. 1565–1640)

This tiny piece is found as No. 194 of the celebrated Fitzwilliam Virginal Book, a manuscript copied originally by Francis Tregian the younger while in prison in the Fleet for recusancy from 1609–19. Today it can be seen in the Fitzwilliam Museum, Cambridge. In the same manuscript are found the magnificent variations by Farnaby 'Up Tails All' which we discussed in *Form and Meaning*, Units 15–16 of the Arts Foundation Course,[1] and which were played on the gramophone record accompanying those units.

Giles Farnaby was a fairly typical Renaissance composer insofar as he fits comfortably into the picture we have attempted to draw in Unit 17 of musicians in Renaissance society. Born about 1565, Farnaby graduated Bachelor of Music at Oxford in 1592, contributing to Thomas East's psalter which was published the same year. In 1598 Farnaby's set of twenty four-voice canzonets (madrigals) was published. However, Farnaby is probably best known as a composer of keyboard music.

Incidentally, since no keyboard music was published in England before *Parthenia* of 1612–13 (a collection of twenty-one pieces by Byrd, Bull and Gibbons) we must rely on manuscript copies for keyboard music of before that date. Where several manuscript copies of the same piece exist these very often differ in detail and occasionally in substance too. Usually it is possible to rely on one 'prime' source for the basic text, although in a critical edition the variants are collated and the information given in a critical commentary. The Fitzwilliam Virginal Book, though a collection of unique importance, nevertheless does not always provide the best texts. Yet in Farnaby's case it is entirely responsible for his reputation as a keyboard composer, for of his fifty-three pieces fifty-one are found in no other source. The Fitzwilliam Virginal Book also contains pieces by Richard Farnaby, Giles' son.

Short though *Giles Farnaby's Dream* is, it nevertheless falls into three distinct sections (each of which may be repeated). Because of this, and because the piece is also in common time, it is, in fact, a miniature pavan. **Play side 2 band 1 of your record.** I think that three things are fairly obvious. First, the

[1] The Open University (1971) A100 Humanities: A Foundation Course, Units 15–16 *Form and Meaning*, The Open University Press.

music is extremely smooth and restful, as befits dream-music. Next, it has a continuous tune and a subordinate accompaniment. Third, it has a strong sense of direction; it does not wander.

EXERCISE

Can you give musical reasons for the somewhat subjective statements I have just made? That is:

(a)   Why is the music restful?
(b)   Why does the tune stand out so well?
(c)   Why has the piece a strong sense of direction?

SPECIMEN ANSWER

(a)   The music is restful because all three elements – melody, harmony and rhythm – are themselves smooth. More precisely, the melody or tune moves mostly by single steps, that is by adjacent notes with few leaps. The only big leap, at the beginning of bar 7, perhaps even strengthens the overall effect appearing like a deep sigh half-way through. The rhythm is smooth because the piece moves almost exclusively in quavers or eighth notes without any sudden disturbances. The harmony is smooth too, changing slowly with one harmony in the first bar, and elsewhere entirely without dissonance or surprise.

(b)   The tune stands out well because it is very much a right-hand tune – that is, it is well separated from its accompaniment and doesn't become confused with it. The accompaniment is generally confined to the left hand, sometimes lying quite low on the keyboard, and only rarely does it rise sufficiently to get within close range of the tune.

(c)   The piece has a strong sense of direction because the tune's movement is finely controlled. It rises higher in each section, reaching a climax shortly before the end of the piece, after which it subsides to rest.

DISCUSSION

I don't think you need to be a musician to have made somewhat similar observations to those in the suggested answer. There is nothing very technical about them. You may have used different ways of expressing much the same points, of course. Perhaps you found the tune 'graceful rather than angular'; the harmony 'uneventful'; the tune 'singing' and the accompaniment 're-strained'. I don't very much like these expressions however, because you are largely replacing my earlier subjective comments with others of your own, whereas my phrases like 'moves mostly by single steps', 'moves almost exclusively in quavers', 'lying quite low on the keyboard' are all reasonably objective and factual.

There is a great deal more one could say on these three matters. If stepwise movement creates smoothness, if gentle flowing quaver movement does like-wise, then why are there any leaps at all in the tune and why are there three instances of shorter note-values (the semiquavers in bars 5, 9, 12)? We've noted that *Giles Farnaby's Dream* has a strong sense of direction, but is this appropriate to dream music? Shouldn't dream music be vague and meander-ing? The same answer meets both points. Art has its own internal rules of proportion and movement which good artists observe more or less instinctively. Music may create a mood, or even attempt to portray a natural phenomenon, but the moment it allows external influences to dictate its inner life then the chances are it will fail in both respects. Thus there are a few non-stepwise movements in Farnaby's *Dream*, for the simple reason that if there weren't it would be dull. The occasional semiquavers are equally important, for the first two occur at the beginning of each new section to give the extra impetus (like a springboard) that the music requires after the falling cadence in the bar before. The final little flourish of semiquavers in the last bar is one of several melodic and rhythmic formulas of the time and to have avoided it would probably never have crossed Farnaby's mind. Even an insincere writer may find 'Yours sincerely' a successful way to end a letter.

Beethoven (1770–1827) faced this same problem in the *Pastoral Symphony*. He did not intend it to be programmatic, but he went as far as to write headings to the various movements. The first reads 'Pleasant and cheerful feelings aroused when approaching the countryside'. Because he wrote the first movement in sonata-form (as did every other composer of sonata and symphony at that time) the first section of the first movement is repeated. Do we assume, therefore, that precisely the same 'pleasant and cheerful feelings' went neatly round in Beethoven's head a second time as he literally or mentally took a walk that day?

Incidentally, another reason why the music of Farnaby's *Dream* is particularly satisfying (to us at least, if not to his contemporaries also) may be because it shows a keen sense of tonal awareness. Although we can't actually talk of major and minor keys at this time in the history of music, the *Dream* is clearly in D (major or minor). Consequently, when the second section begins in F major our subconscious expectations are in some way fulfilled, because F major is the most closely related key to D minor (they both share the same key-signature of one flat) and in fact, it is called its relative major. (Each minor key has one.) Composers recognized this special relationship and made much use of it during the following two or three hundred years. Maybe some fundamental law is operating here, or maybe we in the twentieth century are simply responding to a musical practice we can hardly have escaped if we've ever listened to the radio and heard classical music – either way, there's something very comfortable and reassuring about Farnaby's second section and the reason for this I feel, may well be a tonal one.

Farnaby's tonal sense is forward-looking and so is his melodic sense. Bach used very much the same pattern of successively rising phrases with a climax about three-quarters or five-sixths of the way through in many of his shorter pieces. Having reached the climax, Bach, like Farnaby, makes the music subside quickly. Farnaby does it beautifully in his *Dream*, by the way – a whole octave of step-wise movement (bars 10–12) before the final cadence with a hint of imitation in the tenor part in the penultimate bar. A further word about imitation. Renaissance music is full of phrases or 'points' that follow each other imitatively – indeed it is part of the essential syntax – and even Farnaby's discreet accompaniment nevertheless contains a certain amount of it. I don't want to analyse this piece to death so will merely observe that the opening three notes of the tune are imitated in the bass in bar 3; that several falling figures in the tune are echoed later in a lower part; and that the last note of the left hand in bar 6 begins a phrase which *anticipates* the tune of bar 7. Perhaps *Giles Farnaby's Dream* is not such a naive miniature as I first suggested, after all!

Please play the *Dream* again, in the light of our discussion. And then, perhaps tomorrow, play it once more without any attempt to 'intellectualize' about it. I hope that your emotive response to this tiny gem will by then be enhanced.

2   Pavan and Galliard: Lord Salisbury by William Byrd (1543–1623)

Dance forms were popular in Renaissance instrumental music, especially the pavan and galliard. The pavan(e) was a stately dance in four-time, the galliard a slightly faster one in three-time. Pavans and galliards are quite often found in pairs – in which case they may well use common thematic material. Each dance was normally in three sections each of which was repeated – although the pair by Byrd we are about to examine is exceptional in that each dance has only two sections. No varied repeats are found notated in the Byrd pair either and in the recorded performance I have improvised them and hope to have given some idea of how such varied or ornamental repeats would have sounded to an Elizabethan listener.

You have heard music by Byrd already and you know something of his life and times. He seems to have excelled in everything he did and it is hardly surprising that his keyboard pavans and galliards are among some of the finest written at home or abroad. There are, incidentally, two outstanding pavan-galliard pairs bearing the title *Lord Salisbury* or *The Earl of Salisbury*, the other pair being by Orlando Gibbons. Both sets may date from around 1612.

EXERCISE

Play side 2 band 6 of your disc and listen to the first 8 bars of the pavan (in fact this section A is, for once, exactly half of the whole piece, which thus has the simplest possible AB sixteen-bar form). Jot down some of the things about the music which seem to you important. I think you should bear in mind the three basic elements of music: melody, harmony and rhythm.

DISCUSSION

You have probably mentioned how smooth and restrained the music is. Perhaps you have used the word 'poise'. Yet it has movement and a strong sense of direction also. The smoothness is achieved by the long melodic lines (bars 1–4 and 5–8) and the largely stepwise movement of the tune; also by the uneventful harmony. The sense of direction is achieved by certain rhythmic devices in both tune and accompaniment and also by tonal means – the cadence on the dominant chord (E major) at bar 8 is quite progressive, in fact, for *c.* 1600, even although no actual modulation has occurred.

Let's look more closely at the points mentioned above. First the tune. It begins with a syncopated or off-beat start to attract your attention (bar 1, first note) and has an interesting contour: up a third, down a semitone (first note of bar 2), then down a fifth and up by step, with a little rhythmic spring ♪. ♪ to the keynote (A); a moment's hesitancy on the note below (last note of bar 3) and confirmation of the keynote (first note of bar 4). Play the opening again on your disc and see how persuasive, both melodically and rhythmically, that opening phrase is.

The second phrase (5–8) presents a little rhythmic motive ♪ ♫ ♩ as a falling sequence, handing it from tune to inner part (6) and tune to inner parts again (7), both the principal melody notes (C B A G♯) and bass of bars 5–8 falling by step. The music subsides to the inconclusive or 'imperfect' cadence at bar 8.

Note the tenor rhythm in bar 1:   ♩. ♪♪ ♩   which recurs in almost the same form in bar 4, and again, in the bass, in bar 8. This is a standard rhythmic formula of the time, especially found in keyboard music. You will note how the harmonic movement is stationary in bars 1, 4 and 8 where these rhythmic motives occur. This dichotomy between movement and rest yields the sense of poise we observed earlier.

EXERCISE

Now play band 7 and hear the second section, B. Please comment on this, in whatever way you like, and when you have done so see if my own remarks are at all helpful either strengthening something you have mentioned, or perhaps pointing out something you have missed.

DISCUSSION

The melody of B comprises three phrases, two short ones (first six notes – beginning with the last note of 8 – next six notes), then one longer phrase (12, last note, to end). The two short phrases have a simple arch form, rising and falling again. The second merely repeats the first an octave higher. The last phrase is more involved, rhythmically, but in essence it falls back to the keynote and uses the same melodic formula

in its last three notes as we heard before in bars 3–4. Incidentally, there is some slight imitation of the treble part to be found in the alto part in bars 9–10.

The stillness of the tune in bars 9 and 11 is compensated for by the movement in the bass. The tonal movement of the piece is interesting and quite progressive. We have already noticed the cadence on the dominant chord of E major at the end of section A. The second section begins in C major – the relative major of A minor, the home key of the piece – and it moves back to A minor during the second half, following three bars (13–15) of essentially dominant harmony (E major chords). This strong, forward-looking tonal sense accounts for much of this pavan's forward movement – to twentieth-century ears at least.

Before you hear the whole pavan, let us consider the galliard which follows it. Two things are clear: the melody is once again a stepwise one; and the music has a cheerful rhythmic drive. First the tune. In the section A, a longish phrase

(1–4) is followed by two short sequential phrases (4–6, 6–8). In section B, there are two longish phrases, the first almost entirely moving by step, the second also largely stepwise. The rhythm makes a good deal of use of the

figure ♩. ♫ ♩ (bar 1, left hand imitated in bar 2 right hand; bars 1½–2½ and 3 middle voice; bar 6 left hand, and modified in 7 and 8. Similarly in B, bars 9, 10, 12, 13).

There is a degree of subtlety about this rhythmic figure which you may not have noticed. It is deliberately ambiguous, for

can be read either as

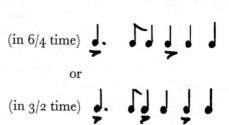

(in 6/4 time)

or

(in 3/2 time)

and there isn't a right or wrong answer. This built-in ambiguity, yielding either two or three main beats to the bar is analogous to some of those ambiguities of perspective – where for example a cube at one moment appears to be a solid, but a moment later becomes void, depending on whether you 'read' its corners as approaching or receding. The eighteenth-century courante, a dance-form much used by Bach and his contemporaries, makes considerable use of this particular device.

A word or two about thematic unity in this pavan and galliard. Though not obvious, it exists. In the first bar of the pavan the dominant rhythm is ♩. ♫ ♩ This same rhythm is stated three times at the beginning of the galliard:

Furthermore, the most memorable part of the opening phrase of the pavan is probably the little rising figure ♫ ♩ and it is this same rising figure, rhythmically expanded to ♩. ♪ that is dominant throughout the galliard. Also, the melody that begins in bar 4 of the galliard and continues through to the first note of 6

is virtually the melody of section B of the pavan:

Incidentally, the second section of the galliard begins with the opening three-note motive ♩. ♪♩ (or ♩. ♪♩ in halved note-values) inverted, that is upside-down. Look at the opening three notes of bars 5 and 9 and you will see what I mean.

Listen now to the whole of the pavan and galliard on band 2.
Remember that I'm playing ornamented versions of the repeats: thus each dance has the form AA'BB'.

3   Prelude and Fantasia by Orlando Gibbons (1583-1625)

There is no doubt that the keyboard music of Orlando Gibbons (1583–1625) was very popular in his lifetime and for quite a while after his death. Over fifty sources of it survive, half of them dating from before 1650. This is several times more sources than survive for the keyboard music of any other of his English contemporaries. Unfortunately not a single note of *any* of Gibbons' music survives in his own autograph despite the fact that as many as ten *secondary* sources survive still for a single keyboard piece, a Prelude in G major. This prelude appears in an early eighteenth-century manuscript along with the words 'This . . . was a favourite lesson [piece] for upwards of a hundred years'.

You have already met one of Gibbons' vocal pieces, the madrigal *The silver swan* – another 'hit' incidentally, since it has remained a favourite in every madrigal group's repertoire for three and a half centuries. Gibbons was one of those fascinating men who come at the end of an era and, Janus-like, look forwards and backwards at one and the same time. He was brought up in traditional circumstances. His father was a member of the Cambridge waits or civic musicians, his elder brother was organist of King's College Chapel, Cambridge, and Orlando himself was a choirboy there under his brother. By the time Orlando was twenty-one he was an organist of the Chapel Royal. He later became private harpsichordist to James I, and in 1623 Organist of Westminster Abbey. Two years after this last appointment he died of an apoplectic stroke at Canterbury where he had been supervising the musical arrangements for the arrival from France of Charles I's bride Henrietta Maria. There is a memorial tablet to him in the north aisle of the nave of Canterbury Cathedral.

Gibbons thus grew up on the traditional fare of English church music of the previous generation and his natural mode of expression was the highly developed sixteenth-century contrapuntal style. But Gibbons was progressive too. He was the first English composer to set only English words in his church music – that is to say he set no Latin. Furthermore, in a work such as the verse anthem *This is the record of John* he showed, in his declamatory word-setting and bold melodic lines, an awareness of the new Italian music:

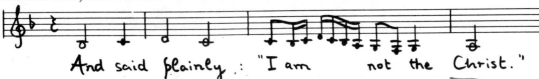

Six of his keyboard pieces appear in *Parthenia* of 1612–13 – 'the first musicke that ever was printed for the virginals'; and when in around 1619 nine 'string fantasies' were published 'the like not heretofore extant' the newness and originality of the music were indeed startling. Thurston Dart, in 'The Printed Fantasies of Orlando Gibbons' (*Music and Letters*, October 1956), concluded that they were the earliest violin music printed in England and contained some of the earliest trio-sonatas composed in Europe.

The prelude and fantasia we are going to examine are not related in their original sources, but nevertheless make a convenient pair and each admirably demonstrates the best of its own genre. I play both on the organ because the fantasia was particularly associated with the Church. The prelude could have been played by Gibbons on either organ or harpsichord, however.

There are only two of these brilliant toccata-like pieces in Gibbons' surviving output (the other being the Prelude in G already mentioned) but I know of no other keyboard music of the period, English or continental, which has such drive and successful inevitability. Perhaps this was the piece John Hacket heard Gibbons playing when in company with some French envoys (in connection with the preliminary arrangements for Charles I's marriage) he entered the 'Door of the Quire' of Westminster Abbey and heard the organ 'touch'd by the best Finger of the Age' – that of Orlando Gibbons. (Quoted on p. 40 of E. H. Fellowes' book *Orlando Gibbons*.)

Will you play the Prelude on band 3 and follow the score at the same time? You will note that the music flows more or less continuously (with a small lessening of movement around the middle, bars 17–21) with rapid semi-quaver movement in one hand while the other has slow-moving chords for the most part. The right hand leads, but shortly after the slowing-up just mentioned, the left hand takes the lead for several bars (25–32) while the right has the chords. The right-hand part then assumes the lead until the end.

I hope you will agree that this prelude displays brilliance and drive. Again, these words are used in the context of music of the period: obviously one could find greater brilliance, in terms of technical demands on the player, harmonic language, range of keyboard, speed, and so on, in Chopin's studies, but Chopin (1809–49) lived in a period when the bounds of musical expression were being rapidly expanded and he himself was a great innovator and virtuoso performer. To compare Gibbons with Chopin is to compare say, St Paul's Cathedral of *c.* 1700 with the Eiffel Tower of 1889 – a futile endeavour, since the media, function, and social context are totally different.

Let us examine the prelude a little more carefully. It begins with left-hand chord and a delayed right-hand entry. The right-hand part falls in semiquavers for about an octave and a half, rises again (bending back on itself in the process) and then deliberately halts the flow by breaking into crotchets at bar 3. This pattern is repeated in sequence in bars 4–5. You don't need to read music to see what I'm talking about, because one of the good things about staff-notation (unlike tablatures) is that the actual 'shape' of a melodic line, its 'rising' and 'falling', is immediately apparent to the eye. After these two halting starts, the music tries again, more successfully, but it isn't until bar 9 that the relentless torrent of semiquavers really begins. The highest note reached is top A

(first note of bar 12)

and this climax goes hand-in-hand with a discord in the left-hand part (the tied note in the tenor)

which forms a classic example of 'preparation, suspension and resolution' (on weak, strong, and weak beats respectively), which we identified in the Introduction to Unit 17. It's all too easy, by the way, when writing music with a great deal of movement to resort to rather purposeless 'note-spinning', but I think you will agree that Gibbons does not fall into this trap.

In bars 17–21, where the movement lessens, the tension and interest is maintained by a new figure – partly rhythmic, partly melodic – which is treated in imitation. Thus the rising figure DEF in bar 17 alto

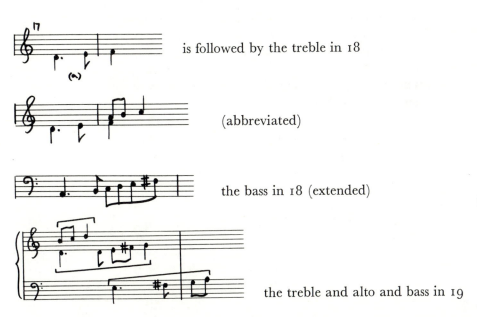

is followed by the treble in 18

(abbreviated)

the bass in 18 (extended)

the treble and alto and bass in 19

and so on. The motive is nicely extended in the bass in 20–21 to prepare the way for the new right-hand movement beginning in 22 – which begins with the same stepwise rising figure in semiquavers (diminution); a coincidence? I doubt it. Here are the bars I've just mentioned:

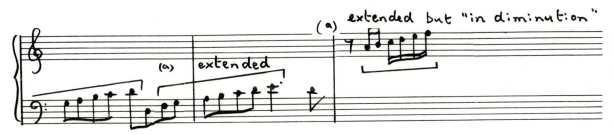

EXERCISE

Following the score, can you find three examples of sequence (sequential patterns) in bars 24 to the end? (N.B. No need to write any music out unless you want to: just mark your score in pencil.) Confirm your ideas by playing the disc.

ANSWER

24½–25 both hands

l.h.   26–28
r.h.   28½–30
r.h.   34–35
r.h.   36¾–38¼

both hands   39–41

DISCUSSION

Maybe you regard this kind of searching as musical nitpicking. In a sense it is – but only in the sense that one has to train oneself to look and listen carefully so that after a while one can make pertinent observations easily and naturally. The point of the above exercise is to show that this music is strongly sequential, a point any professional musician (and a good many other people) would have hardly thought worth mentioning, since it is obvious. But it is worth mentioning, for the sequential method of construction is useful for a composer when writing a sort of piece like the prelude that hasn't any pre-determined form to accommodate it. A pavan or a galliard, for example, has such a form. A free-flowing prelude hasn't, and this is why Gibbons has combined, very skilfully in my opinion, rhythmic interest (opening bars, right hand) sequences (never too long, and well-varied) and counterpoint or imitation (half-way through) in nicely balanced degrees. The result is a purposeful piece of music, not a meandering note-spinner. Now play the prelude again.

You may remember Thomas Morley's definition of a fancy (fantasy, fantasia, fantazia, and other spellings) which we quoted in Unit 17. He described it as the 'most principal and chiefest kind of music' and referred to the composer taking a 'point' of imitation and wrestling with it at his pleasure. Writing in 1597 Morley was quite right, but he could hardly have foreseen the enormous popularity which a further development of this form would have in the seventeenth and eighteenth centuries and beyond – namely, the fugue, a form (or more correctly, a structure) we associate particularly with J. S. Bach (1685–1750) and his contemporaries.

The fantasia we are going to examine by Orlando Gibbons falls into two parts though there is no actual break in the music: a fairly strict opening section, very imitative; and a second half which is almost a prelude of the sort we've just been considering. Indeed, the thematic material of our prelude bears close resemblance to that of this second section of the fantasia, although as I've already mentioned, there is no evidence to show that these two pieces were ever related.

The 'point' which Orlando Gibbons wrestled with and in my opinion made much of, is this one:

not, in itself, a startlingly original idea (though composers of his day were less concerned with originality than today's) but nevertheless with considerable potential. See how the note-values decrease in each of the three bars. Note too, how it has an interesting arch-shape: up and down again with a flick in its tail. Combined, these two simple elements make a unit of great strength. **Listen to band 7: you will hear this point played alone, and then, after a few seconds pause the opening ten bars of the piece** with this point overlapping itself in a restless, nervous manner. It doesn't even get a chance to be heard alone (as Bach's fugue subjects always are) because Gibbons starts the second entry in bar 2, after only the first note of the original point. This overlapping, a device used in later sections of Bach's and other men's fugues is called 'stretto' (close, narrow) and was used to heighten the tension and maintain the listener's interest.

EXERCISE

Band 4 contains the complete fantasia. Will you follow it closely as far as bar 45 (where the florid, semiquaver movement begins) and see if you can hear six more 'entries'. (There are 14 in all, but discount the first three in bars 1–8 please.) Follow the score and mark them in as you hear them. There is no need to put a bracket around the whole entry, just identify the first two or three notes as I have done when first identifying the point. Not every point starts on the same beat of the bar, or even with precisely the same note-values, incidentally. The music would be very dull if it did.

ANSWER

My answer obviously looks rather clinical, but remember I'm identifying all eleven remaining points by numbers, so to speak:

		bar	voice or part		bar	voice or part
Entry Nos.	4	$14\frac{1}{2}$	bass	9	$30\frac{3}{4}$	bass
	5	$17\frac{1}{2}$	treble	10	37	bass
	6	$22\frac{1}{2}$	treble	11	$38\frac{1}{2}$	treble
	7	$23\frac{1}{2}$	alto	12	$39\frac{3}{4}$	bass
	[7a	26	treble 1st note missing]	13	$40\frac{1}{2}$	alto/tenor
				14	$41\frac{3}{4}$	bass
	8	26	bass			

DISCUSSION

Notice how the points or entries become tighter, closer together, as the music progresses. Notice too, how there are consistently three voices or contrapuntal parts. This is thus a 'three-part fantasia'.

EXERCISE

Play band 4 again, this time concentrating on bars 45 to the end. In the light of our discussion so far of both prelude and fantasia, say what seems to you of importance in the construction of the second half of this fantasia. In other words, *what* is Orlando Gibbons doing; *how* is he handling *what* material. Be straightforward and non-technical by all means, and be as brief as you can.

SPECIMEN ANSWER

The second half of this fantasia comprises a fast-moving section with semiquaver interest alternately in right and left hands, and a final tail-piece or coda, slower-moving and itself containing one brilliant flourish (66–67) before the final cadence. The construction of the first of these two sections is very much the same as in the prelude: alternately right-hand and left-hand movement, largely sequential.

Now listen to the whole Prelude and Fantasia on band 4, following the score at the same time. You will surely agree that this music is just as well organized as the music in other forms which we have discussed and that there is much of the 'art which conceals art' in it. Yet in performance it is the purely musical rather than the constructional elements which hold our attention – and this is as it should be. Good composers seldom allow composing techniques to intrude upon the planned effect of their music.

Let us stop for a moment and consider the keyboard instruments an English musician of Gibbons' time would have had at his disposal. The English harpsichord would have had a compass of about four and a half octaves (the modern grand piano has seven and a quarter octaves) and like the piano, only one keyboard. It would have had probably two sets of strings, one of eight-foot pitch, the other four-foot pitch. The plectra would have been of quill. The virginals had a single set of strings of eight-foot pitch, again with quill plectra. The clavichord was never as popular in England as in Germany, but I have played the Farnaby piece on it so that you may hear another Renaissance sound[1]. (The clavichord increased further in popularity in the seventeenth and eighteenth centuries in Germany and was a particular favourite of Bach, by the way.) The English organ was often small having a handful of stops and only one keyboard. There were a number of two-manual organs, however, having a dozen or more stops in all. A particularly fine builder in the early years of the seventeenth century, and one whose work Byrd and Gibbons would have known, was Thomas Dallam who built the instrument at King's College Cambridge in 1606 and at Worcester Cathedral in 1613–14. Dallam's pipework exists still and its purity and clarity of tone confirm what we have observed more generally about Renaissance sonorities.

4   Variations: Mein junges Leben hat ein End'
(My young life has come to an end)
by Jan Pieterszoon Sweelinck (1562-1621)

Figure 16 Sweelinck (Mansell Collection).

[1]   Much amplified, however

In view of the high opinion of the English virginalists' best sets of variations expressed in Unit 17, it may seem odd to have chosen a set by a Dutch com-composer for discussion here. There are good reasons however. First, we discussed the splendid set *Up Tails All* by Giles Farnaby in the Foundation Course and I played these on the disc which accompanied the written material. Many of you will therefore know a set of English variations of the period already.

If you haven't taken the Foundation course, it is still possible that you have studied Units 13–14, the music section of Units 15–16, and the accompanying record, before embarking on these present music units. If not, you will nevertheless find, in these beautiful variations by Jan Pieterszoon Sweelinck (pronounced 'Svaylink') many of the characteristics of the English virginalist school as exemplified by men like William Byrd, Thomas Tomkins, Peter Philips, John Bull, Giles Farnaby and Orlando Gibbons. Two of these composers emigrated to the Netherlands: Peter Philips in 1590 and John Bull in 1613. Bull, renowned as perhaps the greatest keyboard virtuoso of his day, settled first in Brussels, where Peter Philips was one of his colleagues in the service of the Archduke. In 1617 he became organist of Antwerp Cathedral.

Philips and Bull were almost certainly both acquainted with Sweelinck: various cross-references occur in their works. Sweelinck, renowned as performer, composer and teacher, lived in Amsterdam and hardly ever travelled except on brief business trips to other parts of the Netherlands. He was particularly receptive to external influences however, and was clearly influenced by the English virginalists' style, characteristics of which occur with increasing frequency throughout his keyboard compositions. Sweelinck was also a splendid composer of vocal music – nevertheless we probably value him most highly as an instrumental composer.

Today, when communications are easy and widespread, it is easy to forget how vital actual personal contact was between teacher and pupil, and one colleague and another – expecially if such colleagues were from different artistic environments yet each pre-eminent in their field. Thus to credit Bull with influencing Sweelinck is entirely reasonable. To credit Sweelinck with influencing Bach, born some fifty years after Sweelinck's death, may seem far-fetched yet it is nevertheless plausible. Among Sweelinck's pupils were nearly all the leading North German organists – the three principal posts at Hamburg were held by his pupils and Samuel Scheidt at Halle (Handel's birthplace) was yet another. Now it was these North German musicians who were a formative influence in J. S. Bach's development (and initially, Handel's too) and it is no idle theory therefore, to regard Sweelinck as one of Bach's musical grandparents. And remember, Sweelinck's art contained seeds from England. An interesting thesis subject might well be to trace these in Bach's music. (Bach and Handel had greatly differing formative years, by the way; Bach, like Sweelinck, travelling little and being essentially a parochial musician, Handel on the other hand, travelling widely and absorbing new influences and subordinating them to his own genius wherever he went. Bach would have been a dull composer if his mind had been as parochial as his body, but by studying foreign music – English, French and Italian – and by corresponding with foreign musicians, he was able to bring much the same raw-material as Handel as grist to his own creative mill.)

I think it entirely appropriate therefore, to take as our example of Renaissance instrumental variations this set by Sweelinck. To quote Willi Apel: 'Sweelinck's Variations on *Mein junges Leben hat ein End'* are among the dozen truly great masterpieces in this genre. An unusually attractive theme is presented with an astonishing exuberance of ideas, which often change within one and the same variation.' Furthermore, the theme itself, a gallows-song, is German, presumably given to Sweelinck by one of his pupils – so we can find in these variations elements from Dutch, English and German art.

Here is the tune. Play band 9 and listen to it.

NB. The sign :‖ means repeat this section. Thus the overall form is AABB.

> Mein junges Leben hat ein End', mein' Frewd' und auch mein Leyd:
> Mein' arme Seele sol behend scheiden von meinem Leib:
> Mein Leben kan nicht lenger stehn, 's ist schwach, führwahr es musz vergehen, es fehrt dahin mein Leyd.

(Free translation:

> My young life is at an end, my pleasures and also my sorrows:
> My poor soul must soon leave my body:
> My life's strength can last no longer, it is weak and surely it must pass away, and with it my pain.)

The overall form of this memorable tune is AABB. Yet it is more subtle than this, for A comprises two phrases, the falling step wise phrase (a) and a shorter cadential phrase (b). B comprises three phrases: a new *rising* stepwise movement phrase (c) which is repeated (and which incidentally starts and ends on the dominant of fifth degree of the scale, contributing substantially to the tune's sense of purpose); and the original cadential phrase (b) to round off the whole tune.

Thus the complete scheme is A   A   B   B
                             ab   ab   ccb   ccb

which contains plenty of 'unity-with-variety', a characteristic of folksongs and an essential element also of most 'high art'.

Another reason why this tune may have appealed so much to the progressive Sweelinck is that it happens to have a built-in tonal ambiguity: although phrase (b) is 'in D minor', what about phrase (a)? This could be either in D minor or its relative major, F major; it could even be harmonized as a mixture of the two. (Such consideration doesn't apply to the unaccompanied folksong but only to a sophisticated harmonization of it.) This in fact is what Sweelinck does in his initial harmonization of the theme. **Play band 10** and see if you can follow this. He begins phrase (a) in D minor but ends it in F major. Phrase (b) follows, but in the repeated version of (a), bars 4–6, he begins (a) in D minor again and ends it in D minor. Thus we find a deliberate dichotomy in the Sweelinck harmonization well suited to the sombre life-and-death mood of the original song.

EXERCISE

Before we consider individual variations, play band 5 and listen carefully to the whole set. Afterwards, jot down below some of your reactions.

DISCUSSION

Perhaps you remarked on the cumulative effect of the piece and the lessening of movement just before the end. Perhaps this struck you as a reflection of the text: the young man's sorrow, tension, and death. Maybe you found the piece rather fussy, with a lot of movement but little real development of the kind you are used to in later music. The rapid movement at times may have struck you as inappropriate, or worse still, mere note-spinning – 'effect without cause' as Wagner (1813–1882) once said of some music he disliked.

I am guessing at your reaction of course, but let me comment on my suggestions. The cumulative effect of the music, it seems to me, is self-evident and is something that you find in many, if not most sets of variations by composers of any generation. Farnaby's *Up Tails All* displays this characteristic, so do Brahms' *Variations on a Theme of Paganini* – although both Farnaby and Brahms, since they are writing more variations than Sweelinck, make their climax occur in stages with restful variations in between. The same cumulative effect is observed by most jazz improvizations – which after all, are essentially variations on a recurring harmonic bass or 'ground' (a term Renaissance composers frequently used and which remains valid today). So Sweelinck isn't doing anything exceptional in this respect. He's merely going through the normal motions. What about the slowing-up in the final variation however, in particular at the beginning of it? This again is in no way exceptional. Farnaby did it at the beginning of his last variation, and so have countless other composers. It's like a speaker taking a deep breath before making his final point. It adds weight. Sweelinck harmonizes the beginning of his last variation rather severely and poignantly however, and I think this is likely to be a deliberate reminder of the essential sadness of the song.

If you found the music fussy I would agree with you to this extent: Renaissance keyboard style is busy-sounding to modern ears insofar as composers took advantage of the potentialities of the extremely flexible sixteenth-century instruments and clearly delighted in 'muscle-flexing' of a type which had not been possible on earlier ones.

Furthermore, slow chordal music does not sound as well on plucked keyboard instruments (harpsichord, virginals, spinet) as on the later piano, so ornamentation of melodic and bass lines, broken chords (arpeggios), repeated notes, and all movement of this kind are especially suited to the instruments for which Renaissance composers wrote. Sometimes the fingers get the upper hand over the mind and composers succumb to the temptation of display as opposed to genuine musicianship. I don't think Sweelinck succumbs in that way in these variations however – although there are plenty of instances among his lesser contemporaries.

As far as development is concerned, if you found a lack of this you would also be right to a certain extent. The sort of development we find in eighteenth- and nineteenth-century composition is largely tonal – that is, the music changes keys (alters its centre of gravity) to achieve heightening and lessening of tension and to maintain a sense of purpose and direction. In addition it may rely on increasing dynamic effects – it may get louder and orchestrally richer. Neither of these devices is found beyond a rudimentary stage in Renaissance music. The development such as it is, is almost entirely conceived in terms of movement and texture. Faster movement is generally more exciting; heightened tension can be achieved either by having more movement in one or more parts, or by using richer texture – more parts in close imitation. In all probability the Renaissance composer will use these devices in combination.

So you may have been expecting development of a kind Sweelinck never knew or used and this is hardly his fault, but rather a matter of listening technique. One has to try to listen to early music in its own terms and, at times, forget about later music. In its own terms Sweelinck's piece has a perfectly logical development.

If you were merely indifferent to *Mein junges Leben hat ein End'*, there's not very much I can do to help, except to ask you to bear with me while I take you through the variations pointing out some of their characteristics, after which I hope you may feel more positively – and favourably – towards the music.

Let us now consider these variations in some detail.

Figure 17 The opening bars of Mein junges Leben hat ein End, *in a contemporary hand. Not autograph. (Berlin, Staatsbibliothek, MS. Ly. A1, p. 166.)*

We shall count Sweelinck's opening music as variation 1 rather than a mere statement of the theme since it clearly has all the characteristics of a variation. Note too, that we count the first *complete* bar as bar 1.

Sweelinck states the theme clearly in the top part with only one momentary variant of the basic tune – in bar 7 where

In other words he delays the top note G and when it sounds, after a quaver rest (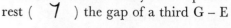) the gap of a third G – E

is filled in with the 'missing' note F.

This little figure is 'imitated' in the alto

one beat later, and the tenor a beat after that:

The lower parts of section A (bars 1–8) are smooth and flowing, but two things are worth noting. In bar 4, the end of the phrase we earlier called (a) and the closing phrase (b) are stitched by movement in the middle parts:

but this stitching is done constructively, for it is no other than the tune (a) itself anticipating its repeat in the melody thus:

Simple, but effective – the 'art which conceals art' in fact. The bass part is silent from bars $4\frac{1}{2} - 6\frac{1}{2}$, but when it enters it has a rising five-note figure:

which turns out to be an anticipation of (c), the opening melody of section B (bar 9):

A coincidence? Possibly, but I doubt it. Sweelinck is giving his material a strong sense of unity, probably quite deliberately. **Listen to the first 8 bars again on band 10.**

Now let us consider the remaining bars of variation 1, bars 9–20. These are slightly more involved and contain rather more imitation. The melodic phrase (c) beginning

is accompanied by a descending figure

in the left hand, and this descending figure is imitated two beats later in the right hand

So far so good. But (c) is also found, slightly modified, in the bass:

and a moment's thought will lead us to the conclusion that the descending figure

can be regarded either as (c) inverted (upside-down) or, more likely, as a reminder of the opening phrase of the whole piece

in shorter note-values or in *diminution*, as we say. Sweelinck's first variation is thus beginning to show a truly remarkable unity in its material. (Of course, Sweelinck must have realized this potential of the folksong the moment his pupil showed it to him.) The rising bass in bars 14–15 is again the figure (c), though syncopated, (that is, with displaced accent) and anticipates the melody of bars 15–16. I could point out further imitation, but that is sufficient to indicate the way Sweelinck's mind was working.

Listen now to the whole of variation 1 on band 11.

Variation 2 begins in 'close' imitation:

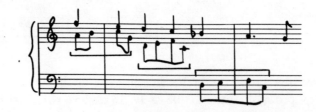

with a small four-note figure tumbling down through the alto, tenor and bass parts. This figure, slightly modified, occurs elsewhere too, in bars 22–23, in the left hand first

and then in the right

The original tune stands out clearly in the treble or soprano part. The same tumbling effect is pursued in the repeat of section A of variation 2, but this time all four parts are involved in a chain of 'suspensions' – that is, of discords and their resolutions. At the beginning of section B, the left hand has the rising figure (b) first, and the right hand follows. Note that the original figure

has been abbreviated to

In bar 30 bass and tenor lead in thirds – chords whose notes are a third apart – thus:

and in bar 32 the original tune

(last note of phrase (c) first note of phrase (b)) is stitched by an upwards flourish of sixths:

and this is followed in 33 by a similar flourish of thirds in the left hand. At 35 the tune

becomes

and this decorated version of (c) is exactly copied an octave lower in 37–38.

The cascade of thirds in the left hand at 39 are an extension of the rising thirds and sixths idea previously noted, and further descending flurries occur in both hands in 39–40. More movement of this kind means development in Sweelinck's terms and thus the effect of variation 2 is to heighten the sense of tension inherent in variation 1. **Now play variation 2 on band 12.**

New ideas abound in variation 3. It begins in two-part texture, the original tune in the top part being accompanied by a nervous semiquaver figure in the alto part. On closer scrutiny, this semiquaver figure turns out to be a livelier version of the opening figure of the previous variation.

Thus

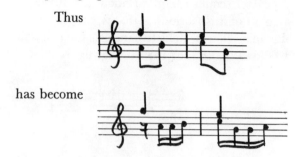

has become

and this figure tumbles downhill as the slow-moving tune falls too, in its opening phrase, and the left hand picks up the figure when it enters at 42. Instead of repeating this idea when the phrase (a) of the tune is repeated, Sweelinck turns his attention to the tune, and modifies that in an exciting way. The first note of each group of four semiquavers is the tune proper, but the intervening semiquavers give it a new character. In 46 the tune is almost lost in the flurry of the semiquaver and sextuplet (six-note) movement. But it is still there as you can see from the asterisks:

Listen to this much of variation 3 on band 13. Next Sweelinck does a relatively rare thing in keyboard music of any period, though something which his English colleague John Bull frequently did; he uses repeated notes to liven up the tune.

Thus the phrase

becomes

which you may feel is not a very clever way of developing his material. Perhaps that's why Sweelinck doesn't pursue the repeated-note idea, but continues the semiquaver movement throughout the next few bars in a more purposeful manner, passing it from the right hand to the left, and then in bar 55 involving both hands at once. As if he hasn't introduced enough new material, Sweelinck introduces yet another new figure in 58:

Listen now to the whole variation on band 14.

EXERCISE

Several new ideas emerge in variation 4. **Play variation 4 on band 15 and see if you can identify the two most prominent ideas.** How do you think they contribute to the development of the piece so far?

SPECIMEN ANSWER

Variation 4 begins with a long-short-short rhythm (♪♫ ♪♫♪♫

etc.) in the right hand, the tune nevertheless still prominent, and when this figure is passed to the left hand in 62–64 the original melody tops the right-hand

chords. This figure ♪♫♪♫ is a prominent one. It is followed by

some fairly active semiquaver movement and a dotted ♪.♩♪.♩

figure, but the second important figure in the variation is introduced at 75

and lasts to the end. It is a triplet figure, ♪♪♪ ♪♪♪ a flowing,

lilting figure that involves both hands and creates a smooth-flowing texture and is relaxing after the rather hectic movement that has gone before it. In less technical language, the piece has shown a gradual increase of movement up to variation 4 bar 74, and now it becomes momentarily relaxed, perhaps in readiness for further development.

In variation 5 the figure ♪♫ of variation 4 is restored, but this time

appears in a chain of thirds (bars 80–81) and continuous semiquaver movement takes over in 82. The consecutive thirds and sixths of bars 82–83 are again very characteristic of John Bull (and they are very awkward to play). The broken chords or 'arpeggios' in the left hand of bars 84–85 and the accompanying right hand chords give a splendid sonority. In the remainder of the variation a variety and combination of motives occur: rushing semiquavers in both hands simultaneously (86–88); left hand semiquavers (89–90); thirds and sixths (right hand of 91–93); curious-looking broken chords (95–96); continuous left hand semiquavers (97–100). This variation is not recorded separately.

The final variation opens with four remarkable bars. Composers of Sweelinck's day were not very adventurous harmonically, so when they do write something unusual it is worth examining it closely. Bar 101 has four right-hand chords over a single note in the bass. The first and third chords are consonant with the bass E, but the second is dissonant and the third curiously rich for Sweelinck's time. There is only one bass note in the next bar too, but Sweelinck does something very subtle. The bass note F acts as a 'pedal', that is it sustains several harmonies above (as the E did in the previous bar). One would expect bar 102 to be firmly in F major, since the bass is in F and the tune has three notes of the common chord of F in it.

i.e.

(expected harmonic basis of bar 101)

However Sweelinck harmonizes the third chord as a D minor chord and to anyone tonally sensitive this is disturbing. He meant it to be I'm sure, for he again avoids the obvious in bar 104, where the first chord would normally be D minor; he has instead the 'interrupted' chord of B♭ major. Incidentally, the original tune is being imitated one bar later in the alto in 101–103 thus:

More activity occurs in 105–107 (♪♫ ♪♫ used imitatively), but from 109 to the end the movement slackens despite some moving imitation. For example the right-hand tune in 109–110 is followed at 110½ in the tenor. The bass line beginning with the last note of 110 has the outline of the original phrase (a) and the semiquavers in the bass beginning with the last beat of 112 echo (in diminished form) phrase (c). Section B of the final variation is exactly repeated, incidentally, the only occasion in which this happens. Perhaps it underlines the stillness and sadness of the young man's fate, I'm really not sure.

Now play band 5 again and hear the complete set of variations. I hope you will think the enthusiasm that I have shown for the music is justified.

APPENDIX I REFERENCES AND FURTHER READING

1   Histories

(a)   General Histories

Lang, P. H. *Music in Western Civilization*, Dent, 1942, £5·25.
As its title implies, this large-scale work discusses music against its cultural and historical background.
Harman, Alec, and Mellers, Wilfred *Man and His Music. The Story of Musical Experience in the West*, Barrie and Rockliff, 1962, £3·50.
Part I deals with Medieval and Early Renaissance music (up to 1525); Part II with late Renaissance and Baroque music. There are some 130 pages on secular, sacred and instrumental music in the late Renaissance. Many music examples.
Grout, D. J. *A History of Western Music*, Dent, 1966, £5·25.
Perhaps the best broad introduction to music history.

(b)   Renaissance Music

Hughes, Dom Anselm, and Abraham, Gerald (eds.) *The New Oxford History of Music, Vol. 3: Ars Nova and the Renaissance, 1300–1540*, Oxford, 1960, £3·50.
Of relevance to these units are Chapters XII (*The Instrumental Music of the Middle Ages and Early Sixteenth Century*, by Yvonne Rokseth) and XIII (*Musical Instruments*, by Gerald Haynes*.)
Abraham, Gerald (ed.) *The New Oxford History of Music, Vol. 4: The Age of Humanism, 1540–1630*, Oxford, 1968, £7·00.
Of relevance to these units are Chapter II (*The Sixteenth-Century Madrigal*, by E. J. Dent), IV (*Solo Song and Cantata*, by Nigel Fortune) and VI (*Latin Church Music on the Continent–2: The Perfection of the a Capella Style*, by Henry Coates and Gerald Abraham). Chapter II contains sections on Monteverdi, Marenzio, the Madrigal in England, Byrd, Morley, Weelkes and Wilbye, Byrd, and Gibbons and Tomkins; Chapter IV contains sections on the English Ayre, Dowland, Campion and Rosseter; Chapter VI deals with Palestrina and Lassus.
Reese, Gustave *Music in the Renaissance*, Dent, 1954, £4·50.
The standard work on this subject: of most use to those who know something of the music already. Chapters VIII and IX, dealing with the sacred and secular music of the late Renaissance, are particularly relevant.
Robertson, Alec, and Stevens, Denis, (eds.) *The Pelican History of Music, Vol. 2: Renaissance and Baroque*, Penguin, 1963. 37½p.
This volume of the Pelican History of Music contains a necessarily rather compressed account of Renaissance Music.

(c)   Music in England

Blom, Eric *Music in England*, Penguin, 1942.
A readable and not unduly technical account of English music in its historical and social contexts. Very short.
Walker, Ernest *A History of Music in England*, 3rd ed. revised J. A. Westrup, Oxford, 1952, £2·75.
The standard history of English music.
Young, Percy M. *A History of British Music*, Benn, 1967, £5·25.
A more recent study.

2   The social and literary background

Lowinsky, Edward E. 'Music in the Culture of the Renaissance'. *Journal of the History of Ideas*, XV (1954), 509–553.

Mackerness, Eric *A Social History of English Music*, Routledge & Kegan Paul, 1964, £2.10.

Pattison, Bruce *Music and Poetry of the English Renaissance*, Methuen. 1948, £1.80. A very useful book. Some chapter headings: 'Music in Sixteenth Century Society', 'Musical and Poetic Forms', 'The Madrigal', 'The Air'. Bibliography of both contemporary and modern works.

Pattison, Bruce 'Literature and Music in the Age of Shakespeare', *Proceedings of the Royal Musical Association*, LX (1933–4), 67–80.

Stevens, John *Music and Poetry in the Early Tudor Court*, Methuen, 1961, £3.15. A study by the editor of *Musica Britannica, Vol. XVIII: Music at the Court of Henry VIII*. In three parts: *Music and Poetry, Courtly Love and the Courtly Lyric*, and *Music at Court*.

Westrup, J. A. *An Introduction to Musical History*, Hutchinson's University Library, 1955, 52½p. The author, in his preface calls this 'an attempt to outline some of the problems which historians and students have to face, and to give some idea of the conditions in which music has come into existence.' Some chapter-titles: *The Scope of Musical History*; *The Social Background*; *The Influence of the Church*; *Patronage*; *The Musician and his Environment*.

Woodfill, W. L. *Musicians in English Society from Elizabeth to Charles I*, Princeton University Press, 1953, £7.00.

3   Printed collections of source material

Lafontaine, H. C. de (ed.) *The King's Music, 1909.* A transcript of documents relating to music and musicians, 1460–1700, in the Lord Chamberlain's Records in the Public Record Office.

Rimbault, Edward F. (ed.) *The Old Cheque-Book of the Chapel Royal*, Da Capo, 1966, £4.20. The documents of the Chapel Royal, 1561–1744.

Strunk, O. *Source Readings in Music History*, W. W. Norton & Co. New York, 1950, £6.20. Now also available in five paperback volumes of which the third deals with the Renaissance.

4   Performing Renaissance music

Dart, Thurston *The Interpretation of Music*, Hutchinson's University Library, 1954, 57½p. A lucid and provocative introduction to textual and performing problems of early music.

Donington, Robert *The Interpretation of Early Music*, Faber, 1963, £6.30. This invaluable guide to the performance of early music is mainly concerned with music of the Baroque, but there is nevertheless much useful material on Renaissance music, and a valuable bibliography.

5   Renaissance treatises on music

Morley, Thomas *A Plain and Easy Introduction to Practical Music*, modern edition by Alec Harman, Dent, 1952, £2.25. This treatise, first published in 1597, is basically a counterpoint text-book, but it also incidentally sheds much light on the musical life of the late sixteenth century.

6   English church music

Fellowes, Edmund H, *English Cathedral Music*, new ed., revised J. A. Westrup, Methuen, 1969, £3·00.
A study of the English Cathedral repertoire. Devotes one third of its length to chapters on music and the Reformation and on sixteenth-century composers.
Le Huray, Peter *Music and the Reformation in England*, 1549–1660, Jenkins, 1967, £3·15.
Relates changing forms and styles of English music to the events of the English Reformation.
Stevens, Denis *Tudor Church Music*, Faber 1966, £2·25.
A short study, tracing 'the stylistic changes and developments from 1485 to 1603'. Stevens' aim is 'to discuss the music rather than the men who wrote it, and to provide a survey of the period as a whole instead of concentrating on either the Henrician or Elizabethan periods'. Chapters on History and the Liturgy, and on the various *genres* of church music of this period. Bibliography of available editions of the music.

7   The Madrigal

Arnold, Denis *Monteverdi Madrigals*, B.B.C. Music Guides, 1967, 25p.
Fellowes, Edmund H. *The English Madrigal Composers*, 2nd. ed., Oxford, 1948, £1·75. The standard work on the English madrigal. Part I discusses the madrigal in general terms, while Part II has chapters and sections on individual composers.
Fellowes, Edmund H. *The English Madrigal*, 5th ed., revised by J. A. Westrup, Oxford, 1969, £3·00.
Fellowes, Edmund H. *English Madrigal Verse*, 3rd. ed., revised by F. W. Sternfeld and D. Greer, Oxford, 1968, £4·50.
The words of all the English madrigals and lute-songs.
Kerman, Joseph *The Elizabethan Madrigal: a Comparative Study*, Oxford, 1965, £2·75.
A comparison of the English madrigal with its Italian prototype, written by the present Professor of Music at Oxford. Attention is given to the poetry, as well as the music, of the English madrigal.

8   Keyboard instruments

Kirby, F. E. *A short History of Keyboard Music*, Collier-Macmillan, 1966, £4·20.
A history of keyboard music to the present day. Chapter One deals with the history and construction of keyboard instruments; Chapter Two with keyboard music to the end of the sixteenth century. No very detailed discussion of Sweelinck or of the English Virginalists. The bibliography (completed in late 1964) is extensive, covering available editions of the music as well as books and articles on keyboard music.

9   Musical instruments in the Renaissance

Baines, Anthony (ed.) *Musical Instruments through the Ages*, Penguin, 60p.
A compilation of chapters on various instruments and families of instruments. Of special interest to these units are the chapters on the viols and on the Harpsichord (by Thurston Dart) and the chapter on the Harpsichord, Spinet and Virginal (by Raymond Russell).

Paganelli, S. *Musical Instruments from the Renaissance to the 19th century*, Hamlyn, 1970, 90p. A good text supported by seventy excellent colour photographs. Very good value.

10   Studies of individual composers

Byrd
Fellowes, E. H. *William Byrd*, Oxford, 2nd. ed., 1948, £2·10.
A comprehensive study of Byrd's works, with two chapters of biography. The standard work.
Gibbons
Fellowes, E. H. *Orlando Gibbons and his Family*, Oxford, 2nd. ed., 1951.
A short, mainly biographical account.
Marenzio
Arnold, Denis *Marenzio*, Oxford Studies of Composers, 1965, 87½p.
A short monograph on Marenzio's music.
Monteverdi
Arnold, Denis *Monteverdi*, Dent (Master Musicians), 1963, 82½p.
A highly readable 'Life and Works' in Dent's excellent 'Master Musicians' series.
Arnold and Fortune (eds.) *The Monteverdi Companion*, Faber, 1968, £3·15.
A compilation of chapters on various aspects of Monteverdi's music by a variety of scholars. Not very much, unfortunately, on the early madrigals, though there are some fascinating chapters on the later ones and on Monteverdi as opera-composer.
Palestrina
Coates, H. *Palestrina*, Dent (Master Musicians), 1938.
Another of the 'Master Musicians' series.
Roche, J. *Palestrina*, Oxford, 1972, 90p.
A scholarly and lucid introduction to Palestrina and his music.

APPENDIX 2   EDITIONS OF MUSIC

1   Complete editions

Palestrina: *Le opere complete di Giovanni Pierluigi da Palestrina*. Edizione fratelli Scalera, Roma, 1939 – in progress.

Monteverdi: *Tutte le opere di Claudio Monteverdi*, ed. G. Francesco Malipiero; 17 vols.

Vols. 1–10 contain the madrigals and canzonets.

The Lute Song: *The English School of Lutenist Song Writers*. Transcribed, scored and edited from the original editions by E. H. Fellowes, London, 1920–32, 32 vols.

Revised ed. 1959 in progress.

The English Madrigal: *The English Madrigal School*, ed. E. H. Fellowes, London, 1913–24, 36 vols.

Revised ed. 1956 – in progress.

Sweelinck: Opera Omnia, Vol. 1, fasc. III. Keyboard Works and Works for Lute, ed. Frits Noske, Vereniging voor Nederlandse Musiekgeschiendenis, 1968, £9.25.

2   Relevant volumes of Musica Britannica

V – *Thomas Tomkins. Keyboard Music*, ed. Stephen D. Tuttle, 1955, £4.00.

VI – *John Dowland. Ayres for four Voices*, transcribed by E. H. Fellowes and edited by Thurston Dart and Nigel Fortune, 2nd. ed., 1963, £2.50.

IX – *Jacobean Consort Music*, ed. Thurston Dart and William Coates, 2nd. ed., 1962, £4.20.

XIV – *John Bull. Keyboard Music I*, ed. John Steele and Francis Cameron, 1960, £4.50.

XIX – *John Bull. Keyboard Music II*, transcribed and edited by Thurston Dart, 1963, £5.25.

XX – *Orlando Gibbons. Keyboard Music*, transcribed and edited by Gerald Hendrie, 2nd. ed. 1967, £3.12½.

XXIII – *Thomas Weelkes. Collected Anthems*, transcribed and edited by David Brown, Walter Collins and Peter Le Huray, 1966, £4.63½.

XXIV – *Giles and Richard Farnaby. Keyboard Music*, transcribed and edited by Richard Marlow, 1965, £3.75.

XXVI – *John Jenkins. Consort Music of four Parts*, transcribed and edited by Andrew Ashbee, 1969, £7.00.

XXVII – *William Byrd. Keyboard Music I*, transcribed and edited by Alan Brown, 1969, £6.25.

XXIX – *Peter Philips. Select Italian Madrigals*, transcribed and edited by John Steele, 1970.

3   Other available editions

(a) *Keyboard Music*

The Fitzwilliam Virginal Book, ed. Fuller Maitland and Barclay Squire, 2 vols; Dover, 1963, £5.00.

Twenty-four Pieces from the Fitzwilliam Virginal Book, transcribed and edited by Thurston Dart, Stainer and Bell, 1958, 38p.

'A selection of pieces (for the most part, short and not very difficult) by Richard

Farnaby, Martin Peerson, Peter Philips, Edmund Hooper, Robert Johnson and others'.

Parthenia, by William Byrd, John Bull and Orlando Gibbons, transcribed and edited by Thurston Dart, Stainer and Bell, 1962, 63p.

Bull: Ten Pieces, transcribed and edited by Thurston Dart, Stainer and Bell, 43p.

Byrd, William: *My Ladye Nevells Booke of Virginal Music*, ed. Hilda Andrews, Dover, 1963, £5.00.

Byrd: *Fifteen Pieces from the Fitzwilliam Virginal Book and Parthenia*, transcribed and edited by Thurston Dart, Stainer and Bell, 1957, 38p.

Giles Farnaby: Seventeen pieces from the Fitzwilliam Virginal Book, transcribed and edited by Thurston Dart, Stainer and Bell, 1957, 38p.
Contains *Giles Farnaby's Dream, His Rest, His Humour, Farnaby's Conceit*, etc.

Gibbons, Orlando: *Nine Organ Pieces from* MUSICA BRITANNICA, *Vol. XX*, transcribed and edited by Gerald Hendrie, Stainer and Bell, 1967, 50p.

Gibbons, Orlando: *Eight Keyboard Pieces from* MUSICA BRITANNICA *Vol. XX*, transcribed and edited by Gerald Hendrie, Stainer and Bell, 1967, 50p.

Morley: *Keyboard Works*, transcribed and edited by Thurston Dart, 2 vols., Stainer and Bell, 1959, 86p.

Tomkins: Fifteen Dances, transcribed and edited by Thurston Dart, Stainer and Bell, 38p.

Tomkins: Eleven pieces from the Mulliner Book, transcribed and edited by Thurston Dart, Stainer and Bell, 18p.

Tomkins: Nine Organ Pieces, transcribed and edited by Thurston Dart, Stainer and Bell, 38p.

Schott's Anthology of Early Keyboard Music: English Virginalists, Schott, 1951, 5 vols., 30p each.
Vol. 1:   Ten pieces by Hugh Aston and Others. (Early sixteenth century).
Vol. 2:   Twelve pieces from *Mulliner's Book* (*c.* 1555).
Vol. 3:   Seven virginal pieces from B.M. Add MS 30486 (All anonymous).
Vol. 4:   Pieces from the Tomkins Manuscript. (Pieces by Tomkins and Gibbons).
Vol. 5:   Fifteen pieces from Elizabeth Rogers' Virginal Book (1656).

Style and Interpretation, Vol. 1: Early Keyboard Music (1): England and France, ed. Howard Ferguson, Oxford, 80p.
Contains notes on points of interpretation and performance, and some examples of English sixteenth-century keyboard music, as well as examples from seventeenth- and eighteenth-century French music.

Early German Keyboard Music, Vol. 1, *Early French Keyboard Music*, Vol. 1, *Early Italian Keyboard Music*, Vol. 1, ed. Howard Ferguson, Oxford.
An excellent series, inexpensive (all under £1), good texts with notes on interpretation and performance, beautifully produced. The German volume has the Sweelinck variations in it.

(b)   *English and Italian Madrigals*

Marenzio, Luca: *Ten Madrigals for Mixed Voices*, ed. Denis Arnold, Oxford, 1966, 85p. Madrigals by Arcadelt. Clement, de Monte, Rossi and Vecchi.

Invitation to Madrigals, ed. Thurston Dart, Stainer and Bell, 3 vols., 40p each.
A collection of madrigals for varying numbers of parts. Brief notes on the performance of each madrigal.

Invitation to Medieval Music, ed. Thurston Dart, Stainer and Bell, 2 vols., 40p each.

The Penguin Book of English Madrigals, ed. Denis Stevens, Penguin, 1967, 42½p.
A collection of well-known four-part madrigals. Somewhat freely edited.

The Second Penguin Book of English Madrigals, ed. Denis Stevens, Penguin, 50p.

Rediscovered Madrigals: Mixed Voices, ed. Don Malin, Piedmont Music Co., 1969.

APPENDIX 3   RECORDS

1   Church music

ASD 641:   Recital of English and Continental sixteenth-century Church music, including Byrd: *Haec Dies* and Palestrina: *Haec Dies* and *Tu es Petrus*. £2.35.
Choir of King's College, Cambridge, directed by David Willcocks.

ASD 653:   Motets and Anthems, including Gibbons: *Hosanna to the Son of David*, Palestrina: *Hodie Christus natus est* and Byrd: *Hodie beata virgo* and *Senex puerum portabat*. £2.35.
Choir of King's College, Cambridge, directed by David Willcocks.

RG 80:   Gibbons: Seven Anthems, including *Hosanna to the Son of David*, and Evensong for Whit Sunday and Ascension Day. £2.27.
Choir of King's College, Cambridge, directed by Boris Ord, with Hugh McLean (organ).

ZRG 5151:   Gibbons: Voluntaries, Anthems (including *This is the Record of John*) and the *Te Deum* and *Jubilate* from the Second Service in D minor. £2.27.
Choir of King's College, Cambridge, directed by David Willcocks, with the Jacobean Consort of Viols and Simon Preston (organ).

ZRG 5362:   Byrd: *Three-part Mass, Four-part Mass.* £2.27.
Choir of King's College, Cambridge, directed by David Willcocks.

ZRG 5226:   Byrd: Five-part Mass, excerpts from the Great Service and the motet *Ave Verum Corpus*. £2.27.
Choir of King's College, Cambridge, directed by David Willcocks.

ZRG 5436:   Tallis: Church music, including *Salvator Mundi* and the 40-part motet *Spem in Alium*. £2.27.
Choir of King's College, Cambridge, directed by David Willcocks, with the choir of Cambridge University Musical Society, and John Langdon and Andrew Davis (organists).

ZRG 5479:   Tallis: Church music: *The Lamentations of Jeremiah the Prophet*; *Videte miraculum*; Organ Lesson; *Sancte Deus*. £2.27.
Choir of King's College, Cambridge, directed by David Willcocks, with Andrew Davis (organ).

ZRG 5237:   Church music by Tallis and Weelkes. Tallis: *Te Deum* and *In jejunio et fletu*; Weelkes: *Alleluia, I heard a Voice, Nunc Dimittis, Give ear, O Lord, Hosanna to the Son of David*, with organ pieces by Tallis and Weelkes. £2.27.
Choir of St. John's College, Cambridge, directed by George Guest, with Peter White (organ).

ZRG 578:   Palestrina: Motets. £2.27.
Choir of St. John's College, Cambridge, directed by George Guest.

ZRG 620:   Victoria: Mass *O quam gloriosum est regnum*, motets and *Litaniae de Beata Virgine*. £2.27.
Choir of St. John's College, Cambridge, directed by George Guest.

ZRG 5249:   Tomkins: Church music; including the Full Anthem *When David heard that Absalom was slain*, the Verse Anthem *My Shepherd is the living Lord*, and organ pieces. £2.27.
Choir of Magdalen College, Oxford with Christopher Gower (organ), directed by Bernard Rose.

II   Secular music

SXL 6384:   Madrigals by Weelkes, including *Thule, the Period of Cosmography, Cease Sorrows now, As Vesta was from Latmos Hill descending, O Care thou wilt despatch me*. £2.27.
The Wilbye Consort, directed by Peter Pears.

VSL 11078:   Madrigals by Morley and Wilbye, including Morley's *Now is the month of Maying*. £1.69.
The Deller Consort.

TV 34402S: *English Madrigals from the Courts of Elizabeth I and James I.* Contain madrigals from a wide range of composers, including Bennet's *All creatures now are merry-minded* and Gibbons' *The silver swan*. 99p.
The Purcell Consort of Voices, directed by Grayston Burgess.

STGBY 624:   English Secular Music of the Late Renaissance. Contains Weelkes' *Thule, the Period of Cosmography* and *The Cries of London*, and other madrigals and Viol pieces by Vautor, Gibbons and Tomkins. £1.61.
The Purcell Consort of Voices and the Jaye Consort of Viols, directed by Grayston Burgess.

TV 4017:   *The High Renaissance in England.* Sacred and Secular vocal music by Gibbons, Byrd, Morley, with consort and keyboard pieces by Gibbons (Lord Salisbury's Pavan), Tomkins and Bull. 99p.
The Purcell Consort of Voices and the Jaye Consort of Viols, directed by Grayston Burgess, with Simon Preston (Harpsichord and Organ).

ZRG 652:   *I love, alas:* Elizabethan poetry and madrigals. £2.27.
The Purcell Consort of Voices, with Robert Spencer (Lute) and Jeremy Brett (Speaker), directed by Grayston Burgess.

ZRG 572:   *Metaphysical Tobacco.* Songs and Dances by Dowland, East and Holbone. £2.27.
The Purcell Consort of Voices directed by Grayston Burgess and Musica Reservata, directed by Michael Morrow.

ZRG 643:   *The Triumphs of Oriana:* includes Bennett's *All Creatures now are merry-minded*, Weelkes' *As Vesta was from Latmos Hill descending*, and Morley's *Hard by a Crystal Fountain*. £2.27.
The Purcell Consort of Voices with the London Sackbut Ensemble. Elizabethan Consort of Viols and Gary Watson (Speaker), directed by Grayston Burgess.

SAWT 9481:   *English Consort Music, c. 1600–1640.* Contains Fantasias by Byrd and pieces by Lawes and Tomkins. £2.27.
The Leonhardt Consort, directed by Gustav Leonhardt.

SAWT 9511:   English Music for Recorders and Consort of Viols, 16th and 17th Centuries. Pieces by Tavener, Gibbons, Byrd and Morley. £2.27.
The Bruggen Consort directed by Frans Bruggen.

SAWT 9491:   *English Virginal Music, c. 1600.* Pieces by Bull, Byrd, Gibbons and Morley.   £2.27.
Gustav Leonhardt (Virginal and Harpsichord).

TV 342008:   *English Tone-Paintings, Toccatas and Dances.* Includes *The Carman's Whistle* (Byrd), *The Primrose* and *The Fall of the Leafe* (Peerson), *The King's Hunt* (Bull), *The Bells* and *The Battell* (Byrd).   99p.
Sylvia Kind (Harpsichord).

OL 50075:   *Masters of Early English Keyboard Music – Vol. 1.* This volume contains Gibbons' *The Lord of Salisbury's Pavan and Galliard,* and other pieces by Gibbons, Bull and White.   £1.69.
Thurston Dart (Organ, Harpsichord and Clavichord).

OL 50076:   *Masters of Early English Keyboard Music – Vol. II.* Pieces by Byrd (including the pavan and two galliards *The Earl of Salisbury*) and Tomkins.   £1.69.
Thurston Dart (Organ and Harpsichord).

OL 50130:   *Masters of Early English Keyboard Music – Vol. III.* Pieces by Bull (including his *Fantasy* on a theme of Sweelinck) and Locke.   £1.69.
Thurston Dart (Organ)

OL 255:   *Masters of Early English Keyboard Music – Vol. V.* More Bull, including such miniatures as *My self, My grief, My jewel* and *Bull's goodnight.*   £1.69.
Thurston Dart.

SOL 255:   Recital of Keyboard Music by Bull.   £1·69
Thurston Dart.

SXL 2191:   A Recital of Lute Songs. Songs by Dowland, Campion, Rosseter and Morley.   £2.27.
Peter Pears (Tenor) with Julian Bream (Lute).

SB 6646:   Recital of Lute Music by Byrd and Dowland and of Lute-songs by Dowland, including *Wilt thou unkind thus leave me, Sorrow stay* and *In darkness let me dwell.*   £2.50.
Peter Pears (Tenor) and Julian Bream (Lute).

CLP 1726:   A recital of Lute-music by Dowland.   £2.50.
Julian Bream (Lute).

SB 6751:   Recital of Lute-music by Dowland.   £2.27.
Julian Bream (Lute).

198472:   Bull recital by Francis Cameron (Organ), the Koch Gamba Consort and Susi Jeans (Virginals).   £2.35.

RB 659 2:   Recital of Elizabethan vocal and instrumental music including excerpts from Dowland's *Lachrimae.*   £2.50.
The Bream Consort, directed by Julian Bream.

HQS 1249   Two Renaissance dance bands.   £1.60.
David Munrow.

Oryx EXP 46:   The Medieval Sound.   95p.
David Munrow.

HQS 1093:   *Music by Andrea and Giovanni Gabrieli.* Includes A. Gabrieli's *Gloria in Excelsis* and *Benedictus Dominus* and G. Gabrieli's *Buccinate in neomenia, Timor et tremor* and *In eclesiis.*
Ambrosian Singers and Ensemble, Bernard Rose (organ) conducted by Denis Stevens.   £1.53.

GSGC 14072:   *Seventeenth-century music for brass ensemble.* Includes Giovanni Gabrieli's *Sonata pian' e forte* and Matthew Locke's *Music for His Majesty's Sackbuts and Cornets.*
London Gabrieli Brass Ensemble.   £1.49.

839 798LY: *Motets and Madrigals by Gesualdo.* Includes *In monte Olivette, Tristis est amima mea, Tenebrae factae sunt, Luci serene e chiare* and *Ecco, moriro dunque.*
NCRV Vocal Ensemble.

2RG 602:   *Florentine Music.* Pieces by Monteverdi, Marenzio, Cavalieri, Tromboneino (*Io son l'uncello,* which is discussed by Professor Denis Arnold in the radio programme for Unit 19), and anonymous composers. £2.27.

STL 150:   *From the Renaissance.* A four-disc set in the excellent Time-Life Records series. A varied and colourful selection of European music, together with a helpful and lavishly-produced booklet. Only available direct from Time-Life Records.

(We think that although prices of books, music and records will change, their relative costs will remain a helpful guide.)

ACKNOWLEDGEMENTS

Grateful acknowledgement is made to the following sources for material used in these units:

TEXT
R. Bentley & Son for May Herbert (trans.), *The Life of Robert Schuman, told in his letters*; J. M. Dent & Sons Ltd. for D. J. Grout, *A History of Western Music*, G. Reese, *Music in the Renaissance*, P. H. Lang, *Music in Western Civilization* and T. Morley, *A Plain and Easy Introduction to Practical Music*, J. Harman (ed.); Dover Publications Inc. for Sir John Hawkins, *A General History of the Science and Practice of Music*; Faber and Faber Ltd. for O. Strunk (ed.), *Source Readings in Musical History*; L. B. Fisher Publishing Corp. for F. Werfel and P. Stefan (ed.), *Verdi: The man in his letters*; Victor Gollancz for C. Gatti, *Verdi: the Man and his Music*; Heffer and Sons for A. F. A. Keynes, *By-Ways of Cambridge History*; Oxford University Press for E. H. Fellowes, *William Byrd*, J. Kerman, *The Elizabethan Madrigal: A Comparative Study*, D. Arnold, *Marenzio* and Dom Anselm Hughes and G. Abraham (eds.), *The New Oxford History of Music Vol. IV: The Age of Humanism*; Princeton University Press for W. L. Woodfill, *Musicians in English Society from Elizabeth to Charles I*; Rand McNally & Co. for C. Gounod, *Memoirs of an Artist*, A. E. Crocker (trans.); The Royal Musical Association for D. Harris, 'Musical Education in Tudor Times' in *Proceedings of the Royal Musical Association*.

MUSIC
British Museum for Byrd's *Ave verum corpus*, *The Earl of Salisbury's Pavan and Galliard*, Gibbons' *Prelude and Fantasia*, and Morley's *April is in my mistress' face*; Christ Church College Library, Oxford, for Gibbon's *The silver swan* and Monteverdi's *Baci soavi e cari*; Fitzwilliam Museum, Cambridge, for Farnaby's *Giles Farnaby's Dream*; Pendlebury Library, Cambridge for Palestrina's Mass 'Aeterna Christi munera'; Staatsbibliothek, Berlin, for Sweelinck's *Mein junges Leben hat ein End'*.

RENAISSANCE AND REFORMATION